INSIGHT POCKET GUIDES

TORONTO

CITY OF
TORONTO

SKYDOME

D1510831

APA PUBLICATIONS

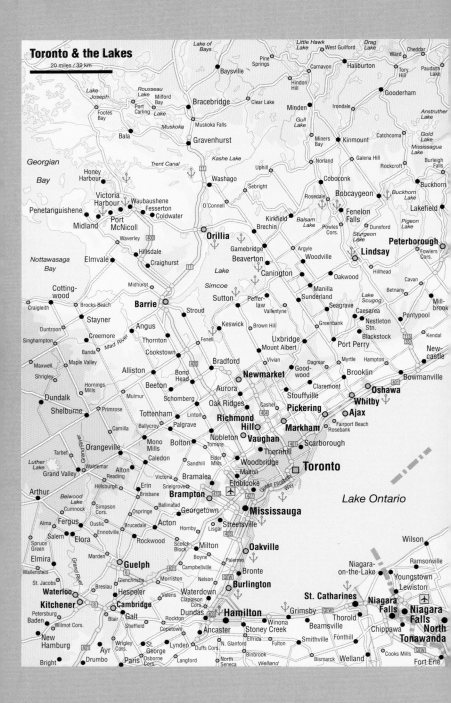

Toronto & the Lakes

20 miles / 32 km

Welcome!

Toronto is a very special city with an unusual history, continually torn between its attachment to the old world and its desire to forge ahead, creating a new world of its own. The result is a successful blend of elements old and new. Toronto has recently been described as 'the most hopeful and healthy city in North America' – which sums up the local spirit which we hope you will discover for yourself.

It is a city rich in museums and theatres, ethnic neighbourhoods and international cuisine, and one that has beaches and islands on its doorstep. It is also an easy city to find your way around, boasting an excellent public transport system. In the following pages our **Insight** correspondent offers detailed itineraries to help make things even easier and to ensure that you get the most out of a brief stay. Most of the suggested routes concentrate on the city itself, but an excursion to Niagara Falls, a priority with many visitors to Canada, could not be left out.

Joanna Ebbutt is an experienced travel writer and editor who has lived in downtown Toronto for eighteen years. During that time she has not only written about Toronto, but also guided countless friends, relatives and acquaintances through the nuances of city life. She is looking forward to sharing the delights of her city with you, acquainting you with its colourful past and offering the kind of practical tips and inside information which will help make your stay a pleasure.

C O N T E N T S

*Pages 2/3:
Toronto's
skyline*

Pages 8/9:
Past and present

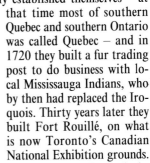

HISTORY &

In The Beginning

Native Indians first settled in the Toronto area around 1000BC, but it was not until Samuel de Champlain, the governor of New France, sent an explorer called Etienne Brûlé to investigate the area in 1615, that the Iroquois village of Teiaiagon was discovered on the east bank of the Humber River. Towards the end of the century, Toronto first appeared on maps, and seemed to cover an extensive part of southern Ontario. The name came from a Huron Indian word meaning 'Place of Meeting'.

Over the years, the French gradually established themselves – at that time most of southern Quebec and southern Ontario was called Quebec – and in 1720 they built a fur trading post to do business with local Mississauga Indians, who by then had replaced the Iroquois. Thirty years later they built Fort Rouillé, on what is now Toronto's Canadian National Exhibition grounds.

With the defeat of the French at the Battle of the Plains of Abraham in 1759, the British became the power-brokers of the Great Lakes region, and in 1787 purchased the land on which Toronto now stands from the Mississauga Indians, in exchange for £1,700 in cash, augmented by goods such as flannel, axes and food.

Trade with the locals

ULTURE

Slowly a settlement grew up around the natural harbour, and in 1790 the construction of Yonge Street commenced, to replace the old canoe route from Lake Ontario to Lake Huron — a simple beginning for what is now the world's longest street, extending 1,900km (1,190 miles) from Lake Ontario to Rainy River, in northern Ontario.

Traditional hunting methods

Quebec was divided into two colonies in 1791 — Lower Canada (today's southern Quebec) and Upper Canada (today's southern Ontario). Initially Niagara-on-the-Lake was the capital of Upper Canada but in 1793, Toronto was renamed York (a tribute to George III's son, the Duke of York) and established as the new capital by Lieutenant-Colonel John Graves Simcoe, governor of Upper Canada. York was chosen because of the potential its harbour offered as a naval station, and its distance from the troublesome Americans. One of the first bills passed by Simcoe's Assembly was to abolish slavery — four decades before it was declared illegal in the rest of the British Empire, and almost 75 years before the United States followed suit.

During the War of 1812, the 700-strong population of York remained loyal to Britain, although the town was occupied twice, albeit briefly, by the Americans in 1813. Today, only the military grid system of streets remains as evidence of Simcoe's times.

One of Toronto's many names, Muddy York, originated during the early 1800s, a comment on the state of the roads at that time. Edward Allen Talbot, a British colonist, described Toronto in 1824 as 'better calculated for a frog pond or a beaver meadow than for the residence of human beings'. Nonetheless, British immigrants were arriving thick and fast. By 1834 the population had increased to 9,252. The first Jewish immigrants began arriving in 1830, mostly from England, Germany, and the US. The seeds of Toronto's later cosmopolitan status were already being sown.

A Growing City

The size and economic stature of York led to it being incorporated as a city in 1834, and renamed Toronto. Socio-economic divisions inevitably occurred, and the old guard, mostly Tories, were constantly being challenged by reform-minded citizens. One result was the disastrously organized Upper Canadian Rebellion in December 1837, instigated by Toronto's first mayor, William Lyon Mackenzie. Due to bad communications and hopeless organization the rebellion failed; fortunately there were few casualties, and life in Toronto soon resumed its normal pace.

Upper and Lower Canada were replaced by the new United Province in 1841, and the capital rotated – in a somewhat unsatisfactory arrangement – between Toronto and Quebec City, until Queen Victoria selected Ottawa as Canada's permanent capital in 1865.

In the meantime, the city continued to grow, and the University of Toronto opened its doors in 1843. Forty thousand Irish immigrants landed in Toronto, driven from their homeland by hunger as a result of the potato famine in 1847. Some continued out west, but many stayed. Despite the first of two great fires, there was a boom in communications generally, through the growth of railways, roads, canals, shipping and telegraph lines during the 1850s. But the city wasn't all about work: baseball made its first appearance in the 1850s, and rowing and horse racing became extremely popular. St Lawrence Hall (Toronto's City Hall at that time) hosted not only major political meetings, but world-renowned entertainers such as Jenny Lind and Tom Thumb.

All this activity culminated in Toronto becoming the capital of the newly created province of Ontario, upon the confederation of Canada in 1867. By 1879 it had its first telephone exchange, with 40 subscribers. The same year, Sir Sandford Fleming invented the concept of Standard Time, while working at the University of Toronto.

Parliament Building

The population grew unabated, as Toronto continued to receive Welsh, German and Irish Catholic immigrants – driven from their homes by poverty – as well as blacks fleeing from slavery in the United States. More Jewish settlers arrived in the 1880s after the massive upheavals in Russia.

'Toronto The Good'

Towards the end of the 19th century, Toronto earned another of its sobriquets. Its loyalty to Queen Victoria and the British Empire, and its firm belief in the sanctity of the Sabbath, lead to its reputation as 'Toronto the Good'. This reputation was solidified by the federally-imposed Lord's Day legislation, which prohibited most working, sporting and entertainment activities. To this day, Toronto is still attempting to shake off that worthy reputation.

There was a spate of designing public buildings, such as Old City Hall and Queen's Park, the provincial legislature, in a massive, ornate Romanesque style, entirely reflecting the belief of Toronto's upper echelons in the natural order of life. But even for the masses, life was improving. Central heating, hot water and indoor plumbing became standard in many homes, and other developments such as the automobile, electricity and high rise buildings began to have an immense impact.

And still the immigrants arrived. Between 1900 and 1911, up to 1½ million people came to Canada, from south and east Europe, as well as from Britain. As with the earlier influx, some went west, but many settled in Montreal and Toronto.

At the same time, the arts were attaining ever-increasing support. The period between 1908 and 1915 saw the establishment of the Toronto Symphony Orchestra, the Art Gallery of Ontario and the Royal Ontario Museum. In the science arena, Dr Frederick Banting's discovery of insulin, while at the University of Toronto, once again put the city on the world stage.

There were few bright spots during the Great Depression of the 1930s. Historic St Lawrence Hall was used as a flop house for several years, and Canadian unemployment reached a horrendous 32 percent. Yet one cultural 'temple' was born in 1931 – Maple Leaf Gardens, a 12,586-seat arena that is still mecca to hockey fans

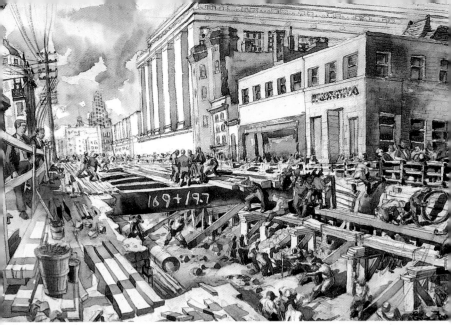

Building Toronto's subway

today. Extremes of weather seemed to match the economic hardships: winters can be bitterly cold, but during a July heat wave in 1936, one wit fried an egg on the steps of City Hall.

After World War II, Toronto the Good's reputation began to show some cracks. In 1947, the first cocktail bars were allowed, despite the howling of outraged critics. A massive increase in the population of Toronto and surrounding areas, caused by fresh waves of immigrants from Europe, resulted, in 1953, in the amalgamation of the city of Toronto with surrounding townships, to become the Municipality of Metropolitan Toronto. The badly-needed subway finally opened in 1954, connecting Union Station to Eglinton Avenue and reducing traffic congestion.

As another sign of the changing times, Nathan Phillips – the man who spearheaded the building of New City Hall – was elected Toronto's first Jewish mayor, in 1955. Another step on the road to liberalisation and cultural freedom took place in the 1960s, when Torontonians were finally allowed to go to movies, plays and concerts on Sundays. It was also said to be in the name of progress, when developers began to tear down everything that stood in the way of their new constructions. But they were met with determined opposition. Battle lines were quickly drawn and although there were some losses, buildings such as Old City Hall, Union Station, Holy Trinity Church and many others were saved from destruction.

Flower-powered youth moved into Yorkville in the late 1960s, squatting in the old and somewhat derelict Victorian homes. In a few years, however, they were ousted, and the buildings were tastefully restored. Ironically, Yorkville is now everything that the flower-children would have rejected, packed with trendy boutiques, galleries, and chic restaurants.

Contemporary Toronto

The last 20 years have seen the city change dramatically. The path was set by the election as mayor, in 1972, of David Crombie. A Conservative reformer, he played a significant role in making the city as livable as it is now. Height limits were set on new buildings, and many century-old houses were renovated in previously poor immigrant areas, such as Cabbagetown. However, this did not create affordable accommodation and subsidized housing in new downtown developments began to appear. Areas such as the St Lawrence Market acquired fresh vitality as a direct result of such developments, which included a healthy mixture of socio-economic groupings.

Unlike many North American cities, Toronto has a vibrant inner core. The downtown population grew by almost four percent between 1986 and 1991, and al-

Cabbagetown's Victorian dwellings

though there are poor neighbourhoods, there are no ghettos, and the crime rate is much lower than in any comparable American city.

In 1989, only 500 parking spaces were installed at SkyDome – the new downtown home for Toronto's baseball and football teams – deliberately encouraging people to use public transport and downtown streets.

The mass evacuation of businesses, and Anglo-Quebecers generally, from Montreal to Toronto, precipitated by French nationalism and the election of the separatist provincial government in 1976, also had a major impact on the growth of Toronto's downtown core. In contrast to Quebec, bilingual street signs began to appear in many of Toronto's ethnic neighbourhoods. The relaxation of federal immigration laws also resulted in the arrival of Asians, Latin Americans, West Indians and Moslems from all parts of the world.

The 1970s and 1980s saw the addition of several major structures that had further impact on the local and global scene, starting with the CN Tower – at 553m (1,815ft) the world's tallest, unsupported structure, and Toronto's most recognizable symbol. In 1979, the Eaton Centre was completed, a $200 million, 6-ha (15-acre) development, with 302 stores on four levels, and ten years later came SkyDome. Despite supercilious snickers from certain elitist corners, all three

The CN Tower

Skyscrapers and sails

entertain and thrill thousands of visitors, year after year, and make a palpable difference to the city's coffers.

There is also a huge creative community – the diversity of Toronto's cultural sector is reflected in newspapers such as *Now* and *Eye*, where there are pages of listings of theatre and literary events, concerts, new gallery showings and more.

In a 1993 survey on 343 North American cities, by the *Places Rated Almanac*, Toronto took fourth place. The factors the cities were judged on included living costs, health care, crime rate, arts and recreation, and climate. Toronto's placement was achieved despite its cool, even cold, winter climate.

The influence of more than 80 different ethnic groups, on a total population of 3.8 million, is immeasurable. Certain signs are obvious, such as the hundreds of restaurants producing cuisine from around the world, but the overall psyche of so many different peoples living together in one city is not easy to measure. How do you gauge acceptance and understanding? The numbers are awesome – over 350,000 Chinese, 400,000 Italians, 100,000 Greeks, 80,000 Poles, besides thousands of Koreans, West Indians, Ukrainians, Tamils, and Vietnamese. During the week-long West Indian Caribana festival, non-stop music pounds away and photos of dancers tucking into curried goat, hot Jamaican patties and pots of chicken at the Toronto Island picnic fill local papers. The days when most Torontonians had British ancestry are long gone. Visitors to Toronto should try a *gelato* in Little Italy, *dim sum* in Chinatown, or *souvlaki* on the Danforth, to appreciate some of the many different cultures.

In October 1993, the Toronto Blue Jays won baseball's World Series for the second year running. The ecstatic celebrations that followed could only have happened here. Thousands of deliriously happy fans crammed Yonge Street, practically from Lake Ontario up to Highway 401, on the northern boundary of the city, yet Metro Police made only 32 arrests – a reflection on the peace-loving inhabitants of Toronto the Good!

Playground pleasures

Historical Highlights

Pre 1600s Entire region inhabited by Native Indians.

1615 Etienne Brûlé, a French explorer, discovered the Indian village of Teiaiagon, on the site of what is now Toronto.

1720 French set up a fur trading post in order to trade with Mississauga Indians.

1750 French built Fort Rouillé.

1759 Defeat of French in the Battle of the Plains of Abraham in Quebec City led to the British becoming the main power in the Great Lakes region.

1787 Mississauga Indians sold the English the land on which Toronto stands.

1793 Town of York is made capital of the recently formed Upper Canada, by its governor, Lieutenant-Colonel John Graves Simcoe.

1812 War of 1812.

1813 Occupied twice, briefly, by Americans.

1834 York is elevated to city status and renamed Toronto.

1837 The unsuccessful Upper Canadian Rebellion instigated by Major William Lyon Mackenzie.

1841 Upper and Lower Canada reorganized as the United Province.

1843 University of Toronto opens its doors.

1847 40,000 Irish refugees arrived in Toronto, as a result of the potato famine.

1867 Toronto becomes capital of the newly created province of Ontario within the confederation of Canada.

1879 Sir Sandford Fleming invented Standard Time at the University of Toronto.

Early 1900s Old City Hall and Queen's Park designed in Romanesque style.

1906 Toronto the Good's reputation solidified by the Lord's Day legislation, which prohibited most working, sporting and entertainment activities.

1921 Discovery of insulin by Dr Frederick Banting, while working at the University of Toronto.

1929 Black Thursday on October 24 heralded the arrival of the Great Depression.

1931 Maple Leaf Gardens was opened, a 12,586-seat ice hockey arena.

1934 Toronto Stock Exchange moved into Canada's first air-conditioned building, at 234 Bay Street.

1939 War was brought close to home when a German torpedo destroyed the liner *Athenia*, killing all passengers including 200 Toronto citizens.

1947 The first cocktail bars were allowed in Toronto.

1954 Hurricane Hazel caused damage worth $25 million, and the death of 81 people. Subway opens, connecting Union Station with Eglinton Avenue

1970s Mass evacuation of Anglo-Quebecers from Montreal to Toronto.

1972 Election of David Crombie as Mayor, a Conservative who played a major role in reforming the city.

1978 Election of John Sewell as Mayor, a radical reformer who continued Crombie's policies.

1990 The completion of Underground City, a 11-km (7-mile) stretch from Union Station to Dundas & Yonge Streets.

1993 Toronto Blue Jays win baseball's World Series for the second year in a row. The city's cultural life is further enriched by the inauguration of the Princess of Wales Theatre, as well as the North York Performing Arts Centre.

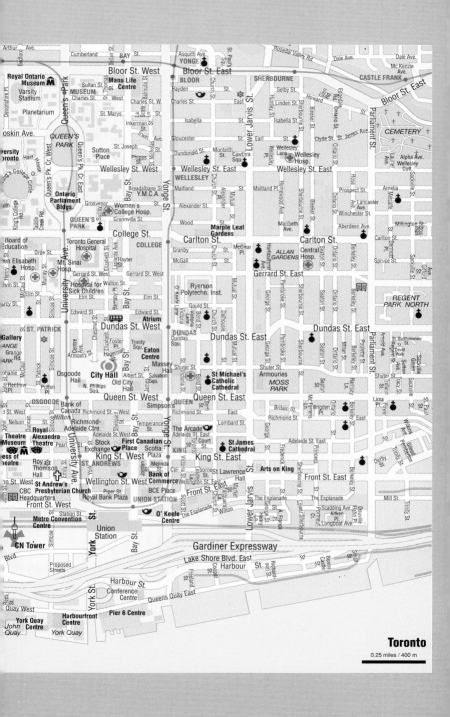

Toronto

0.25 miles / 400 m

The bulk of the explorations described in this book focus on the City of Toronto, one of the six municipalities that make up Metropolitan Toronto. Days 1–3 have been arranged to give you an overall flavour of the city, while the Pick & Mix section allows you to put together your own itinerary. For the excursion to Niagara, aim for an early start.

The TTC Rocket

One of the reasons why visitors enjoy Toronto so much is that it's an uncomplicated city to get around. The city is based on a north–south, east–west grid. From most of the downtown core you can see one of Toronto's most famous landmarks, the CN Tower. It's close to Lake Ontario – the city's southern border – so unless you've lost all sense of direction, you should be able to work out where you are.

Toronto's public transportation system is operated by the Toronto Transit Commission – the TTC – and all the itineraries described here are geared towards a combination of walking and using public transport. The subways are clean, safe and efficient, and since parking downtown can be expensive and difficult, travelling by TTC is often the better way to go – to use their own slogan. For details on special tickets and passes, see *Practical Information*. It's important to remember that you need a ticket, token or the exact change for riding on buses and street cars, as drivers don't carry change.

You need not worry about travelling around Toronto alone. Nowhere mentioned in this guide should give cause for concern. If some other areas interest you, check with your hosts or your hotel. Taxis are usually easy to find, and fares are reasonable.

Greater Toronto Sights

Breakfast at Restaurant Marché Mövenpick before taking a two-hour coach tour of the city, followed by a walk and lunch in part of the theatre district. Nearby, the CN Tower provides an aerial perspective to the morning tour. Finish up with an early evening cocktail at the top of the tower or afternoon tea at one of Toronto's most famous hostelries, the Royal York Hotel.

–To the start: although Gray Line coach picks up passengers from many downtown hotels, breakfast at Marché is a fun, energizing way to begin your first day in Toronto. Take the TTC to King Street subway station. Exit at Yonge Street, south west corner and walk south. Shortly after you have crossed Wellington Street, you come to the entrance of BCE Place. Prices (per person) for the main sights are indicated as follows: $ = under $10; $$ = under $20. All prices given in this guide are in Canadian dollars. Enjoy!–

In a metropolis the size of Toronto, a general sightseeing tour is an excellent way to get a 'fix' on the city. **Gray Line Tours** (tel: 594-3310) operate from the beginning of April to the beginning of December, and tickets ($$) can be purchased from your hotel or from the Gray Line driver. Pick-ups begin almost an hour before the beginning of the actual tour, which starts at 10am, but a convenient pick-up at the Royal York Hotel is only 15 minutes before the tour commences, so aim to be there by 9.45am.

Begin your day with a relaxing breakfast around 8am at Restaurant Marché Mövenpick, in **BCE Place** – designed by

Marché Mövenpick Restaurant

Toronto Sights

0.5 miles / 800 m

The Royal York Hotel

Spanish architect Santiago Calatrava, and one of Toronto's newest and most magnificent downtown developments. From Yonge Street you enter **Heritage Square**, where gaily coloured banners adorn the exterior of the restaurant. Inside, you'll be faced with a buffet-style selection of muesli, omelettes, croissants and muffins. Afterwards, leave BCE Place through the **Galleria**, where a soaring cathedral-styled lobby is flooded with dappled lighting.

Allow 15 minutes to get to the **Royal York Hotel**, to join the bus tour. You will come out of the Galleria on Bay Street, opposite Royal Bank Plaza. Turn left and walk to Front Street. Cross Bay and continue west to the hotel, one block over at the corner of Front and York streets. The hotel has been a Toronto landmark since 1929, with its green copper, château-style roof. Built by Canadian Pacific Railways, at the time it was the greatest and the tallest hotel in the British Empire. Buy a ticket for the tour from the hotel's concierge in the lobby.

On the tour, you will be introduced to many of Toronto's highlights, a number of which you will be returning to, and exploring in more detail, later in your stay. Along the way, you'll receive a potted, anecdotal history of the city and the many and diverse people who have made it their home over the past 200 years.

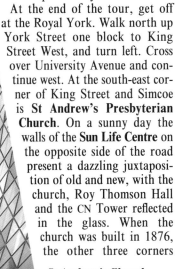

At the end of the tour, get off at the Royal York. Walk north up York Street one block to King Street West, and turn left. Cross over University Avenue and continue west. At the south-east corner of King Street and Simcoe is **St Andrew's Presbyterian Church**. On a sunny day the walls of the **Sun Life Centre** on the opposite side of the road present a dazzling juxtaposition of old and new, with the church, Roy Thomson Hall and the CN Tower reflected in the glass. When the church was built in 1876, the other three corners

St Andrew's Church

Roy Thomson Hall

were occupied by Government House, Upper Canada College (a prestigious boys' school that later moved to another location) and a popular tavern. For a while the corner was known as Legislation, Education, Damnation and Salvation.

On the other side of Simcoe Street, **Roy Thomson Hall** is Toronto's main concert hall – a futuristic-looking building designed by Canadian architect Arthur Ericson. The shining exterior of honeycombed glass encloses a stunningly airy lobby, which in turn encircles the concert hall with its state-of-the-art acoustics. It is named after billionaire newspaper magnate Lord Thomson of Fleet, whose family gave the largest single donation towards its construction. Forty-five-minute tours of the hall ($) are offered at 12.30pm every day except Wednesday and Sunday, depending on concert scheduling.

Now cross to the north side of King Street. The next two blocks, from Simcoe Street west to John Street, are almost entirely Ed Mirvish territory, except for a short cluster of restaurants and bars including **Il Fornello** for terrific pizza, **Peter's Hall of Fame**, a sports bar, and a bar called **Quotes** – check the quotes outside.

Royal Alexandra Theatre

Ed Mirvish's career started with the opening of Honest Ed's (see *Shopping* section) in the 1940s, but he entered the theatrical business with the acquisition in 1962 of the historical **Royal Alexandra Theatre**. Built in 1907, it seemed destined to become another downtown parking lot 55 years later. To the rescue came Ed Mirvish, who spent huge sums of money on restoring the building to its original Edwardian splendour before bringing in the hundreds of first-rate productions which have been staged over the last 30 years. In fact, many of the greatest actors in the English-speaking world have performed on the Alexandra's stage.

Several neighbouring warehouses were then purchased by Ed Mirvish and converted into restaurants to cater to the theatre-going crowd. As it has the most varied menu, I would suggest **Old Ed's** ($). Whichever one of the restaurants you chose, they all feature stained-glass windows, tiffany lamps, gilt mirrors and walls covered with framed autographed photos of the many legendary celebrities who have performed at the Royal Alex.

If you're there at a weekend, check out **Ed's Theatre Museum and Market of the Absurd, Unusual and Ridiculous** (Saturday and Sunday, noon–9pm, free admission) on the second floor of Old Ed's. Everything is for sale, from a six-foot cigar-store Indian and fake fruit to costumes worn by the likes of Maggie Smith, Glenda Jackson and Peter O'Toole. It's an amusingly eccentric collection.

In 1993, Mirvish and his son David opened their third theatre, the **Princess of Wales**, at the corner of King and John Streets. It was built specifically to accommodate the hit musical *Miss Saigon*, scheduled for at least a two-year run. (They also purchased the historic Old Vic, in London, England in 1982.)

At John Street, cross the road and head south towards the CN **Tower** (Monday to Saturday 9am–12am, Sunday 10am–10pm in the summer; Sunday to Thursday 10am–10pm, Friday and Saturday 10am–11pm in the winter, tel: 360-8500) – it's barely a five-minute walk, and you certainly can't miss it.

In case of inclement weather, such as low cloud, postpone your trip until another day. Instead, visit **SkyDome** – see *Pick & Mix Option 3* – or tour the spectacular new **Canadian Broadcasting Corporation** headquarters (free tours Monday to Friday, 3pm, tel: 205-3684) at 250 Front Street West.

Once at the tower, purchase tickets ($$) at the base, which are printed with the time you will be able to go up. There's plenty to divert you at the bottom of the tower including various space age games and attractions. Summer weekends are busiest, when the longest waits are between 11am–4pm, and 8–11pm. On windy days, the elevators are automatically slowed down by roof-top sensors but normally it takes 58

Mirvish Territory

seconds to reach the Observation Deck of this 553-m (1,815-ft) tower (the equivalent of 187 storeys) in elevators with floor-to-ceiling glass walls.

For a couple of dollars more, you can continue up to the Space Deck – at 147 storeys, it's the highest public observation gallery in the world. You may feel the subtle movement of the tower – don't be alarmed, as the (slight) flexibility increases the strength of the structure. On clear days you can reportedly see up to 160km (100 miles), while below, tiny planes take off and land at Toronto Island Airport and toy street cars trundle along King Street. Even Torontonians who have seen them many times before find the views mesmerizing.

Back on the indoor Observation Deck, the **Kodak Mini-Theatre** shows a fascinating 15-minute movie on the building of the tower, including dramatic footage of the bright orange Sikorsky helicopter installing the final section of the 91-m (300-ft) antenna one Sunday morning in March 1975. In fact, the primary purpose of the tower is communications – currently 16 Toronto radio and TV stations transmit to a vast chunk of southern Ontario.

Also on the Observation Deck is **Horizons**, the world's highest bar. Its unparalleled view certainly justifies a drink, especially at sunset or at night. However, you don't need a drink to appreciate the vistas, especially if you venture into the blasting wind on the outside balcony, one floor below the Observation Deck.

Afterwards, take the elevator down and return to Front Street. Turn right and head towards the subway, only five-minutes' walk away. When you come, yet again, to the Royal York Hotel, con-

Union Station

sider splurging on a traditional afternoon tea of wafer thin sandwiches and scones with cream and jam, in the **Acadian Room**.

Otherwise, continue along Front Street to **Union Station**. Built in 1924 in a neoclassical style, the enormous vaulted ceiling of the cavernous ticket hall is based on the baths of Imperial Rome, and early Christian basilicas. Sixty feet (18m) above, the destinations of trans-continental trains are engraved in giant letters around the walls. Union Station has witnessed much of Canada's history, and is still a focal point, being the main station for cross country and local commuter trains, and a subway station.

Exploring Downtown and Harbourfront

Breakfast in Trinity Square beside the Eaton Centre, before a walking tour of downtown's financial district and the historic St Lawrence Market area. After lunch, proceed down to Harbourfront for an afternoon beside the water.

–To the start: take the TTC to Queen Street station, and leave from Albert Street exit at the north end of the platform. This brings you into the food concourse at the Eaton Centre.–

Today you will need comfortable shoes, although there will be plenty of opportunities to snack, browse or shop. On your

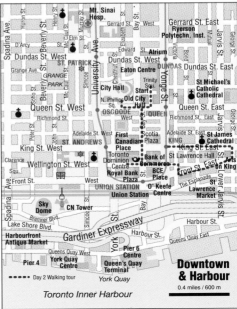

The Eaton Centre

left as you enter the Eaton Centre is **Michel's Baguette**. Pick up a coffee and croissant, then take the escalator and go up one level. Walk straight on, towards the Eaton's department store. Just before you reach the store you come to another escalator. Take this up to 'ground' level, turn left and take the double glass doors marked 'To the Marriott Hotel and **Trinity Square**'.

Old and new blend serenely here, in this small square beside **Holy Trinity Church**. Pick a bench and savour both your coffee and the surroundings. The church was built in 1847, and is now surrounded by the Eaton Centre and a galaxy of shiny new office towers. But you can still hear the birds and be soothed by sounds from the nearby fountain. Two rather whimsical bronze sculptures, *Encounter* and *Neighbours*, add their own somewhat surreal contribution to the square.

The first plans for the **Eaton Centre** included the demolition of Old City Hall and Holy Trinity Church.

City Hall area

Fortunately the uproar that followed the announcement ensured that the plans were overturned. The redesigned Eaton Centre was finally completed in 1979 – a lofty glass palace that unashamedly exposes its pipes, columns and mechanical systems to the world. When you're shopping, look up at the geese in flight, sculpted by Canadian artist Michael Snow. After their installation, he successfully challenged an ill-advised decision by management to drape the geese with Christmas decorations.

Art deco doors

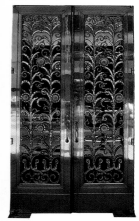

Walk south down James Street (which runs beside the Eaton Centre), cross Salvation Army Square and continue to Queen Street West. To your right is the stately **Old City Hall**, with an intricately detailed frieze on the front facade (including caricatures of councillors who had annoyed the architect, E J Lennox). Built in the 1890s, this was Toronto's third city hall.

Cross Bay Street to **Nathan Phillips Square** and **City Hall**, designed by Finnish architect Viljo Revell – the winner of a competition in which 520 architects from 44 countries submitted plans for this 3.5-ha (9-acre) public area. In summer Nathan Phillips Square (named after Toronto's first Jewish mayor) fairly hops with concerts, a weekly farmers' market, and other festivities, while in the winter the pond becomes a skating rink, especially popular with office workers in their lunch hour. A Henry Moore sculpture, *The Archer*, was a controversial addition to the square in its early years, because it was so expensive.

Now cross Queen Street towards the Toronto Dominion Bank and continue south down Bay Street. There's a wonderful set of art deco bronze doors at 357 Bay Street, and another magnificent doorway at No 320.

Guarding the vaults

As this has been the financial heart of the city for many years, most of the buildings are owned by financial institutions who tended to compete with each other to see who could produce the most outstanding building. This becomes particularly apparent at the corner of King and Bay streets.

First Canadian Place, to your right, is Toronto's tallest building. Designed by Edward Stone, it has a stunning interior of Italian carrara marble halls and striking murals. On the other side of Bay Street is the old **Bank of Nova Scotia** building, another fine example of art deco, while adjacent to it on King Street, the new and lofty **Scotiabank Plaza** has an elegant interior of Italian red granite. The original Banking Hall of the former **Bank of Commerce** (now Canadian Imperial Bank of Commerce) on the south-east corner, opposite Scotiabank Plaza, is worth a look. The **Toronto Dominion Centre** on the south-west corner was Toronto's first skyscraper, built in the 1960s. The black block has a rather utilitarian appearance but when it was built it was considered a decidedly revolutionary design. Further down Bay Street you pass the old **Toronto Stock Exchange**, another splendid example of art deco now cleverly incorporated into the Ernst & Young Tower.

At Wellington Street turn right and walk a short way past **Royal Bank Plaza** on your left, with its 14,000 windows tinted with real gold (always a magnificent sight at sunset), to look at *Pastures*. This group of seated cows created by a Saskatchewan sculptor, Joe Fafard, rests in the shade of the Toronto Dominion Aetna Building, supposedly to remind bankers of their agrarian roots. Inside, there's a collection of Inuit art in the lobby.

Walk back towards Bay and continue east to Yonge Street. Cross the road, turn right and walk down Yonge Street past **Shopsy's**, another Toronto institution, famous for its hot dogs and hamburgers. Turn left on Front Street. The **O'Keefe Centre** (current home to the National Ballet of Canada and the Canadian Opera Company) is on the south side, while the next block houses the **St Lawrence Centre for the Arts**, home of the Canadian Stage Company, which produces some of the city's best dramatic productions.

Just past Scott Street, you come to **Berczy Park**, scene of much of the action during Toronto's annual downtown jazz festival. Immediately opposite on the south side is a row of Victorian buildings occupied by a number of in-

Snatching a nap

Flatiron Building

teresting stores. **Frida** has crafts from all over the world and the **Mountain Equipment Co-op** sells everything you can think of and more for those who love the great outdoors – and the prices are reasonable. Literary types will enjoy **Nicholas Hoare**. With books floor-to-ceiling and comfortable chairs arranged around the fireplace, it's difficult to resist. There are a number of pubs and restaurants in the next couple of blocks, and **Flatiron's** offers a wide assortment of Christmas decorations and other gifts. On the north side of the road is one of Toronto's most photographed buildings, the ever-popular **Flatiron Building**. A triangular shaped brick construction, its west exterior wall, which overlooks Berczy

St Lawrence Market

Park, features an intriguing mural (which windows are real?) by artist Derek Besant.

At 71 Front Street East, look to your left for one of my favourite views – St James' Cathedral framed by Market Square. If you like things French, the café at the corner, **La Maison D'Azure,** is the place to go, and a good potential lunch break after your explorations of the St Lawrence Market area.

Now you're in the heart of an area much loved by Torontonians. There's been a market at the intersection of Front and Jarvis streets since 1803, and the **St Lawrence Market** (Tuesday to Thursday 8am–6pm, Friday 8am–7pm, Saturday 5am–5pm) is still a big draw.

On Saturday, local farmers, including some traditionally-dressed Mennonites, bring their goods to the **North Market** on the north side of Front Street. On both sides of the street, the aisles are packed, as people jostle, eyeing the best cuts of meat and assessing the fresh fish, vegetables, fruit, cheeses, bagels, and much more. The cries of street vendors often mingle with the hauntingly beautiful melodies of South American musicians busking outside.

Toronto's first City Hall was originally housed in the south-side market building. Upstairs in the **Market Gallery** there's a permanent (and free) exhibition on Toronto's history, and a superb view over the market. If a picnic lunch appeals, buy your victuals here, as you'll be reaching a rather charming city park shortly.

Walk north up Jarvis to King Street. On the south-east corner of King and Jarvis is **Arts on King** (169 King Street East), a huge gallery in a restored building where an eclectic selection of Canadian art and craft is on display. The corner building on the south-west corner is the graciously restored **St Lawrence Hall**, Toronto's second city hall. Over the years it has hosted hundreds of gala concerts and banquets, and illustrious celebrities, from opera singer Jenny Lind to P T Barnum's Tom Thumb, have entertained here.

Now head back towards Yonge Street. On the north side of King you come to **St James' Park**, its vibrant flower beds modelled on a 19th-century park, and an agreeable picnic spot to watch the world go by. Beside it is **St James' Cathedral**, a fine example of 19th-century, English Gothic architecture, where there's often a noontime concert. For many years, the 99-m (324-ft) tower was a valuable landmark for ships far out on Lake Ontario. On the other side of King Street is the **Toronto Sculpture Garden**, where there's always something intriguing to ponder over. You can follow the narrow lane on the south side of the garden into **Market Square**, a trendy shopping complex, for lunch at the previously mentioned Maison D'Azure. Or continue along King Street to the regal **King Edward Hotel**, much favoured by visiting dignitaries, for a pleasant and affordable lunch in **Café Victoria**.

From the King subway station (at the corner of Yonge), take the train south to Union Station and switch to the LRT street car which links up below ground with the subway line, for a ride down to Harbourfront.

Irrigation in St James' Park

Now you've arrived at one of Toronto's favourite playgrounds. **Harbourfront Centre** is open year round and puts on an amazingly varied and esoteric program, catering to many tastes. When you get off the street car, **Pier 6 Centre** is to your left. The Toronto Harbour Commission has an interesting exhibition here on the history of Toronto's port, and there's a small café that offers some nifty salads and a patio overlooking the water. Tickets for harbour cruises are sold at a nearby booth.

Harbourfront Centre can occupy the rest of your day and night. There are three main buildings to check out in this waterside park, besides any outdoors activities that may be taking place. The first building, beside the street car stop, is **Queen's Quay Terminal**, (Monday to Saturday 10am–9pm, Sunday 10am–6pm), a former warehouse converted into a specialty store niche – clothing, books, nautical supplies, herbal products and restaurants (three beside the water). It's the sort of place you may end up buying an Aerobic Frisbee for long distance throwing, summer dresses with matching picnic blankets, or an aerodynamically designed bike rack...

Then there's the **Premier Dance Theatre**, where everything from classical to avant-garde dance is performed by Canadian and international dance companies.

At Dockside, around Queen's Quay, harbour cruise ships line up, with names such as *Mariposa Belle* or *Empress of Canada*. Since Harbourfront plays host to a variety of ships all summer long, from tall ships to naval vessels, you never know what you may see.

Tours and t-shirts

The next building to the west is **Power Plant** (Tuesday to Saturday, noon–8pm, Sunday noon–6pm), a former ice-making factory transformed into a gallery for contemporary art, and the **Du Maurier Theatre Centre**.

Beyond the Power Plant, **York Quay Centre** is always a hive of activity. Walk towards the street end of the building and go in through the first set of double doors. This is the **Harbourfront Craft Studio** where 25 self-employed craftspeople make objects in ceramic, glass, textiles and metal. Boards explaining the various processes hang over the work areas. A small crowd usually gathers by the sweating glass-makers

Fishy art

Harbour traffic

at the fiery furnace. At the entrance, **Contemporary Canadian Craft Store** (Tuesday to Friday noon–7pm, Saturday, Sunday and holidays 10am–7pm) sells the artists' work.

At the end of the studio go through the doors to a central lobby where there's an information desk. Do check what's going on as you could easily miss something you'd really like to see. Behind the desk is the **Brigantine Room** where the *Harbourfront Reading Series* (tel: 973-4760) takes place weekly year round. Authors from Canada and around the world come to read from their latest works.

Follow the walkway past the Studio Theatre and the York Quay Gallery (more modern art) to the **Photo Passage**, where thought-provoking work by contemporary photographic artists frequently adorns the curving walls. At the end of York Quay is **Water's Edge Café** and the world's largest artificial skating rink.

A drawbridge over the marina takes you to **Pier 4**. Nautical is the theme here in the various bars and restaurants, and it is also the base for several sailing clubs.

If you're not tired out, the largest collection of antiques under one roof in Ontario is a five-minute walk away. The **Harbourfront Antique Market** at 390 Queen's Quay West (Tuesday to Friday 11am–6pm, Saturday 10am–6pm, Sunday 8am–6pm) sprawls

Watering hole

over two floors. Over a hundred reputable dealers peddle a wide variety of wares, from jewellery to furniture to retouched photographs and prints. Great browsing, even if you're not in the market to buy.

When you've had enough, back-track to Harbourfront for a drink or supper by the water. **Spinnakers** in Queen's Quay offers after-work Oyster Bar specials between 4pm and 6pm, while **Coyote Grill** serves tequilas and sizzling TexMex.

DAY 3

University and Museums

Breakfast on Bloor Street West in the southern Annex; explore the neighbourhood around the University of Toronto; lunch and the remainder of the day at Royal Ontario Museum and the George R Gardiner Museum of Ceramic Art.

—To the start: take the TTC to Bathurst Street Station.—

Bloor Street West, between Spadina Avenue and Bathurst Street, separates the trendy residential area to the north, known as the Annex, from the more colourful, immigrant-based area to the south, inhabited over the years by waves of Jewish, Chinese, Italian and Portuguese newcomers. Consequently, exotic delicatessens mingle with cheap eateries, all offering an enticing variety of ethnic cuisines. Tree-lined streets to the north and south of Bloor Street hint correctly at civilized downtown living.

From Bathurst Street Station turn left towards Bloor Street. Turn left at the corner of Bloor and Bathurst, and there is **Honest Ed's** (see *Shopping* section). Its flashing orange and yellow sign is impossible to miss! The next few blocks reflect the origins and interests of the local residents, including **The Moghul**, an excellent Indian restaurant; **Pauper's**, a pub housed in a former bank, which has a great rooftop patio; and **Lee's Palace**, a popular venue for visiting rock bands. A little further along, you'll come to the **Kensington Natural Bakery and Cafe** (No 460), a potential breakfast spot, and **The Cheese Dairy**, which serves a wide-ranging, loyal clientele. Beyond Borden, on the south side of Bloor, are two terrific book stores, **Book City** and **Longhouse Book Shop** (which only sells books by Canadian authors).

At the corner of Bathurst and Brunswick, is **Future Bakery & Café** (daily 7.30–1am), only an eight-minute walk from Bathurst subway. A Bohemian-style cafeteria with its own bakery at the rear, it serves good coffee and a splendid assortment of muffins and pastries, or you can indulge in a superb omelette, to a background of distinctive but pleasing music, perhaps South American one day, big band the next. An outdoor patio offers waiter service in the summer months.

Leave through the bakery section and turn right down Brunswick, passing the **Poor Alex**

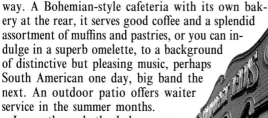

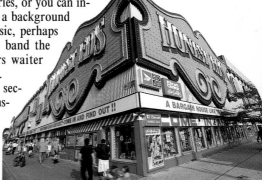

Honest Ed's

Downtown doorway

Theatre, one of Toronto's alternative theatres, and the **Tranzac Club**, haunt of homesick Australians and New Zealanders. Turn left on Sussex, then right on Major. Within five minutes you'll be on Harbord Street, having passed a typical mix of downtown homes, some with stained-glass windows, shiny brass door knockers and colourful flower boxes, others that are somewhat less immaculate.

Turn left on Harbord. Immediately to your left is **The Sound Post**, an unusual store selling stringed instruments and bows, while opposite is **Harbord Bakery**, where Saturday morning visits are *de rigueur* for Annex residents. In the two short blocks between Major Street and **Spadina Avenue** there are five excellent bookstores including two antiquarian booksellers, **About Books** (No 83) and **Atticus Books** (No 84). The more ramshackle **Abbey Bookshop** (No 89) offers a quiet refuge for poets, scholars and pilgrims, while the **Caversham Bookseller** specializes in books on counselling, and the **Women's Bookstore** speaks for itself. One of Toronto's most celebrated restaurants, **Splendido** (see *Eating Out* section) is adjacent to Atticus Books.

Cross Spadina Avenue, and you are now entering the domain of the **University of Toronto**. The large complex to your right is the Athletics Centre. At St George Street, Harbord jigs to the left, and continues as Hoskin Avenue. The rather curious building at the corner of Harbord and St George is the **John P Robarts Research Library**, which is occasionally referred to as Fort Book. The rather fine, turreted building on the northeast corner of Hoskin and St George is the Catholic-based **Newman Centre**.

Although the bus tour on *Day 1* took you through the U of T campus, this is your opportunity to explore it properly on foot. There are also free guided walking tours in the summer (June to August 10.30am, 1.00pm, 2.30pm, tel: 978-5000). Turn down Tower Road at the eastern end of the playing fields, so named for **The Soldiers' Tower** ahead of you, a memorial to the men and women who lost their lives in active service during World Wars I and II.

Beyond the archway, **Hart House** is the late-Gothic, Oxbridge-styled limestone building to your left. The social centre for the university, its **Great Hall** has hosted many famous world leaders. A quote from John Milton on freedom of expression circles the walls. Classical concerts are often held here, while jazz sessions frequently take

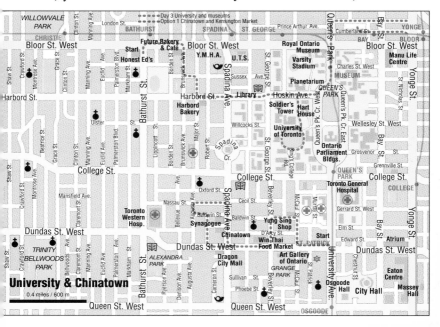

Queen's Park

place in the quadrangle and common rooms. Exhibitions of some outstanding Canadian art are held in rotation in the **Justina M Barnicke Art Gallery** (tel: 978-8398).

In front of Hart House, the **Stewart Observatory** is the oldest building on campus, built in 1814, although it was moved to its current site in 1905. A smashed bicycle beside it is a poignant memorial to Tiananmen Square and the fall of democracy.

Depending on your time and inclination, wander along King's College Circle. West of Hart House is **University College**, a neo-Romanesque building with the first chemistry laboratory in Canada, **Croft Chapter House**. It was known as the 'godless college' after its establishment as a university free from social exclusiveness and religious control in 1853. Next on the Circle is **Knox College**, the Presbyterian theology school, much loved by film and video makers because of its impressive gardens and Gothic architecture.

Backtrack to Hoskin Avenue, cross the road, turn right and go past Trinity College, to **Queen's Park**. The park was named after Queen Victoria in 1860, and is still a peaceful haven in the heart of Toronto. It's a favourite haunt of harried civil servants from the nearby Ontario Legislature buildings, and of thousands of University of Toronto students. Turn left and walk north. Within minutes, you will have arrived at the **Royal Ontario Museum** (100

Chinese exhibits at the ROM

Queen's Park). Admission includes entry to the George R Gardiner Museum of Ceramic Art. If you are feeling hungry, there are many restaurants in the vicinity, but you will save valuable time if you eat at the cafeteria-styled **ROM Café**.

The museum, locally known as **ROM** (Wednesday, Friday, Saturday and Sunday 10am–6pm; Tuesday and Thursday 10am–8pm; closed Monday except during summer, Christmas and March Break school holidays, tel: 586-5551) is the only one in North America to house art, archaeology and science under one roof. Free tours are offered during the day, beginning at 11am with a general tour. The rest focus on specific galleries.

To give your visit to ROM more perspective, visit **Mankind Discovering**, a slightly awkward name for a wonderfully innovative gallery just inside the main entrance. Here the research processes followed by ROM's curators are explained, using certain projects, such as the Kommos Excavation in Crete (on a prehistoric Minoan town) or judging the authenticity of ancient Chinese artifacts, to illustrate the various research stages.

Still on the first floor, ROM's East-Asian collection is world-renowned, and its Chinese collection is one of the finest outside of China. The **Bishop White Gallery** is a stunning collection of temple art, with three huge Chinese wall paintings (painted around AD1300) and 14 massive wooden Buddhist sculptures created between the 12th and 15th century. Even if you know nothing about ancient Chinese temple art, the gallery is awe-inspiring. In the **Ming Tomb Gallery**, a tomb – probably of a mid-17th-century general – is surrounded by enormous stone sculptures from the 14th to 17th century that were excavated from other tomb complexes.

The second floor of ROM is devoted to the Natural Sciences, and the most popular gallery – for children at least – is the **Dinosaur Gallery**. Thirteen dinosaur skeletons are the stars of the show, from the Jurassic period to the rich dinosaur-hunting grounds of Canada's own Badlands in Alberta. The crested hadrosaur **Parasaurolophus** is even mounted in the sandstone block in which it was discovered.

Another well-liked gallery is the **Bat Cave**, a replica of parts of

Dinosaur Gallery

the two-mile-long St Clair Cave in Jamaica. An eerie walk-through is followed by an exhibition on the 900 known species of bats.

The **Evolution Galleries** expand on Darwin's theory and one of the most celebrated exhibits is a coelacanth fish. Known to exist 350 million years ago, they were thought to be extinct until they were rediscovered in the 1930s, and are still being caught by Madagascar fishermen.

The social, technological, historical and artistic development of ancient civilizations are the focus of the third floor. In **The Greek World** there's a spectacular sculpture court featuring 20 classical sculptures from the 4th century BC to the 1st century AD. Other galleries highlight Early Italy and the Etruscans, Bronze and Iron Age Europe, Imperial Rome, Byzantium, Islam, the Ancient Egypt Gallery, and the Nubia Gallery. During term time, you may have to weave your way around school groups, in the Ancient Egypt Gallery especially, but it's worth it. The achievements of these ancient civilizations are astonishing. A personal favourite is the Islam gallery, set up as an Islamic city, in which you can visit the mosque, the shrine, the house, the garden and the market.

Directly opposite ROM is the **George R Gardiner Museum of Ceramic Art** at 111 Queen's Park (Tuesday to Sunday, 10am–5pm, tel: 586-8080). It need not take much of your time, but it is a gem. Free (and extremely informative) tours are offered two or three times a week – the information desk at ROM will have the schedule. It's an intimate museum, with over 2,000 pieces spanning some 3,000 years displayed in eight galleries.

The first floor is devoted to pottery – Pre-Columbian work, 15th- and 16th-century Italian maiolica (tin-glazed earthenware made for everyday use), and 17th-century English delftware. Upstairs, 18th-century continental and English porcelain is on display, including pieces from Augustus II's porcelain factory in Meissen, Germany and a fabulous collection from the Du Paquier factory, Meissen's rival, in Vienna. The Monkey Band, created between 1749 and 1753 by Johann Joachim Kändler at the Meissen factory is enchanting, as are the 18th-century *commedia dell'arte* figurines, including characters such as Pantaloon and Harlequin, produced at both German and English factories.

When you feel you have absorbed as much as you can, you will find the Museum subway station at ROM's main entrance. Or, if you are not too tired or footsore, **Yorkville** (see *Shopping* section) is only a few minutes away for lovers of antiques and teddy bears.

Gardiner Museum piece

Option 1. Chinatown and Kensington Market

Two of Toronto's most vibrant neighbourhoods reside on each other's doorsteps. Together they add up to a full morning of people, food and non-stop hustle. As the tour ends two blocks from the Art Gallery of Ontario, it could be combined with Option 6 to make a full day. For itinerary route see map on page 37.

–To the start: TTC to St Patrick subway station.–

The Chinese are one of Toronto's fastest-growing ethnic groups, and their 350,000-strong community is spread over five Chinatowns. However, this walking tour focuses on the main downtown **Chinatown** – always intriguing, ever frenetic, every day of the week.

From the St Patrick station, start at Global House on the northwest corner of University Avenue and Dundas Street West, and walk west on the north side of Dundas. The street signs are now bilingual, in Mandarin and English. Turn right on McCaul Street, go two blocks to Baldwin Street, then turn left.

This part of Baldwin is a blend of old and new. Besides several popular, European-style restaurants and cafés, there's the **Yung Sing Pastry Shop** (No 22), one of the oldest Chinese pastry shops in Toronto, famous for its tofu and barbecued meat buns, and **Mandell's Dairy** (No 29) – the sole Jewish store remaining on the street and still deemed to sell the best cream cheese in town. **David Ko** both owns the **Chinese Vegetarian Restaurant** (No 39, tel: 599-6855) and organizes excellent walking tours of Chinatown.

Turn left on Beverley Street, then right on Dundas Street. Every other business appears to be a restaurant, and the street is packed with bustling shoppers. Fruit and vegetable stands overflow with all kinds of exotica while in grocery stores such as **Win Thai Food Market** (No 414) the shelves are brimming with endless varieties of soy sauce, snack packets of dried squid and cuttlefish, dried bamboo and lotus leaves. At **Ten Ren's Tea House** (No 454) you might catch a demonstration of the ancient tea ceremony. They sell over 100 varieties of tea – black, green, oolong (a combination of the first two), twig and herbal – priced from $16 to $160 per pound.

If you're ready for a break, visit the café at **All Friends Bakery** (No 492). Moon cakes are one of their specialties, made from white lotus paste, but they also offer a wide variety of rolls, croissants and tarts. It's a favourite stop for local shoppers.

At Spadina Avenue turn right. The sidewalks are invariably crowded, since there are bargains to be had whether you're looking for food, clothing, or leather goods. Just up from Dundas, the **Herbs & Ginseng Wholesalers** (No 289A) is a Chinese herbal dispensary, with a trained practitioner on hand for consultations. Huge jars of dried herbs line the walls, and there are cabinets full of boxes containing hedgehog skins, sea dragons, sea horses, and deer tails – all of which play their role in the healing process.

Backtrack to Dundas, cross the road and continue north up Spadina. **King's Noodle House** (No 296) makes its own noodles, and is renowned for its various barbecued dishes. Wending your way through the crowds, you'll pass emporiums such as **Casa Oriental** and **Tap Phong Trading Company** where you can browse amongst woks, and huge ceramic pots, delicate Chinese screens and much more. At Nassau Street, turn left.

You are now approaching **Kensington Market**. The market really began when Jewish immigrants from central and southern Europe moved here in the 1920s and 1930s. They were largely supplanted in the 1950s by Portuguese incomers, who have since been joined by the Chinese and West Indians.

A Portuguese radio station is at one corner of Nassau and Augusta Avenue, while two fruit markets, operated by families of long-standing in the area, occupy two other corners. Turn left on Augusta and you come to stores selling everything from padlocks and buttons to hats, dresses, used clothing and leather goods. **Fairland** (No 24) is a long-established, family-run children's clothing store that sells name brands such as OshKosh and Alfred Sung at bargain prices.

Much of the joy of visiting Kensington Market is gained from the people you see and the snippets of con-

Chestnuts for sale

Cheerful stall holder

versation you catch. Noisy but cheerful haggling – often in Portuguese – over live chickens and rabbits is more likely to be heard on **Baldwin Street**, one block south, on which you must turn left. Jamaican food is offered at the **Baldwin Royal Food Centre**, while next door, the **New Seaway Fish Market** announces specials such as live carp. Enticing smells waft out from the **Baldwin Street Bakery** (No 191) where sometimes free samples of freshly baked rye bread are offered. **Patty King** (No 187) is an old-time West Indian bake shop where you can taste home-made mango slush or Jamaican-style beef. **European Quality Meat and Sausage** offers the 'best deals in town', while **Madeiro Fish Market** sells West Indian seafood such as kingfish, jack fish and grouper.

Turn right on Kensington Avenue. On your right, the **Global Cheese Shoppe** and **Mendel's Creamery** vie for the attention of cheese lovers, and if you're getting peckish, **Kensington Café** (No 73) offers inexpensive soups, pasta and sandwiches.

Of interest is the **Anshei Minsk Synagogue** (10 St Andrews, tel: 595-5723) down a small street to the left, one block south of Baldwin Street. Built in 1930 in a combination Russian/Romanesque style, it welcomes visitors to services.

Back on Kensington, continue walking south. Closer to Dundas Street, you may feel as though you've stepped back into the 1960s. You'll find vintage Levis at one store, oil and incense at another, and second-hand clothing stores with names like **Morning Glory** and **Tribal Rhythm**.

At Dundas, turn left, and walk back to Spadina. Cross Dundas to **Dragon City Mall** (280 Spadina). In the fast food court at the basement level, ten booths serve Malaysian, Szechuan, Thai, Vietnamese, Singaporean and Indonesian fare. The cries of market vendors competing to attract your attention make it sound more like Hong Kong than Toronto. Seize the opportunity to try fried Chinese redfish pudding, washed down with soya bean milk. It's cheap and cheerful, but if you find the decibel level a trifle high, any of the restaurants I have just mentioned are only minutes away.

Global Cheese Shoppe

Option 2. The Beaches

Much beloved by Torontonians, especially at weekends, The Beaches is a California-style, laid-back neighbourhood known for its Boardwalk, a 20-block promenade beside Lake Ontario; its New England clapboard-and-shingle homes; and Queen Street East, with its eclectic mix of boutiques, book shops, antique stores and cafés.

—To the start: take the No 501 street car east along Queen Street to Woodbine Avenue.—

All you need for a visit to **The Beaches** is time, and comfortable walking shoes. Should you even consider coming out by car, be warned that parking is practically impossible, particularly at weekends. Years ago, The Beaches used to be 'cottage country' for Torontonians eager to escape the hurly burly of city life. Now it's barely a 30-minute ride from downtown. Don't be put off by the dreary approach. It will soon become clear why The Beaches has become one of the most desirable Toronto neighbourhoods in which to live. Somehow, particularly in the summer months, it still feels like a small resort, far from the city.

The Beaches Boardwalk

An Englishman named Joseph Williams was one of the first settlers in the area, in the early 1850s. By 1879 he had created his own pleasure park, **Kew Gardens**, based on its English namesake. Soon, cottages sprang up amongst the trees, and canoe clubs dotted the waterfront. However, it wasn't until the extension of the street car tracks along Queen Street in the late 19th century that 'downtowners' began to descend on The Beaches in droves, to picnic and to dance the summer nights away. Gradually, as the city grew, and transportation improved, the area became a year-round residential area.

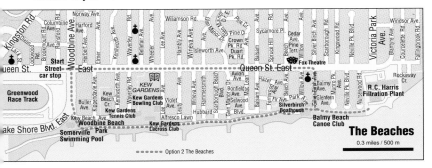

The Beaches

0.3 miles / 500 m

••••• Option 2 The Beaches

Get off the street car just past the **Greenwood Race Track** and walk south down Woodbine Avenue, towards the lake. Go past the **Somerville Swimming Pool** (free admission to its three pools including one Olympic-size) to join the **Boardwalk**. As you turn east, **Lake Ontario** and a wide stretch of sandy beach is on your right, and **Woodbine Beach Park** is to your left. Large, weathered maples stand guard between the Boardwalk and **Trillium Trail**, a narrow biking and jogging path – stray on to this at your peril, especially at weekends, when the Boardwalk and the cycling path are crowded. Dogs on long leashes and small children (unleashed) revel in the freedom of the beach and parkland. On a fine day, sea gulls and Canada geese soar overhead, while sailboats and wind-surfers skim through the waves in an apparently effortless manner.

Soon you'll come to a cluster of community clubs, the **Kew Gardens Tennis Club**, the **Kew Gardens Lacrosse Club**, and the **Kew Gardens Bowling Greens**. There are plenty of benches if you feel like watching for a while. If you cut across to Lee Avenue on the eastern side of Kew Gardens, you will see there's only one house on the west side of the street, No 30. It was built by Kew Williams, son of Joseph (and, yes, named after his father's favourite gardens), as a wedding present for his bride in the early 1900s.

Walk east along Alfresco Lawn to Wineva Avenue, and rejoin the Boardwalk. For a few blocks, the roads extend to meet it. On either side, ancient trees proffer shade to the New England clapboards and the more formal, Edwardian-style brick houses. Many of the street names – such as Hazel, Silverbirch, Pine, Willow, Bracken and Balsam – reflect the area's arboreal origins.

Continue along the Boardwalk, past the **Balmy Beach Canoe Club**. At Silverbirch Avenue, you'll come to the **Silverbirch Boathouse**, where you can borrow volleyball equipment, or shovels and pails for children, at no cost. If you're not ready to leave the water, continue along the sandy beach. Enticing gardens back onto the beach here, and eventually you will arrive at the **R C Harris Filtration Plant**. Built in the 1930s, it's a striking art deco ed-

Ready for action

Leafy suburbs

ifice that has been compared to a Mayan temple. Rising over the lake on a vast, grassy slope, it's an intriguing diversion.

Backtrack to Silverbirch and walk up to Queen Street East. The **Healthy Earth Bilingual Nursery School**, at No 70, reflects the political correctness of many Beaches' residents. Cross to the north side of Queen Street and turn left. Notice the lovely old apartment buildings at Willow and Queen. Fortunately, the blight of highrise buildings has not penetrated The Beaches.

Now it's time for some serious browsing. Start at **Ukukulu** (No 2248) with its lovely Canadian handicrafts. You will pass the **Fox Theatre** at the corner of Queen and Beech. A visit to this movie review theatre followed by a Chinese meal at the **Garden Gate** opposite has been a popular, cheap evening out for Torontonians for decades. Study the unusual mural outside **Quigley's** (No 2232), famous for its Sunday jazz sessions, and check out **Grainfield's Bakery** (No 2222). The smell of the 25 varieties of bread is hard to resist. There's a wide selection of glassware, toys and candles at **Stoneworks** (No 2216).

Cross over to an intriguing cluster of stores on the south side of Queen, including a grotto of exotica at **Legend Arts and Crafts** (No 2359), and an impressive array of boots, hats and other Western paraphernalia at **The Wild Wild West** (No 2357A). Back on the north side, **Babe's Children's Designs** and **The Condom Connection** are unusual neighbours. At **Beadworks** (No 2154) there's a dazzling collection of crystal, Indian glass, Venetian and hand-painted wood beads, offering great potential for creating your own accessories. You can even sign up for a workshop.

By now, chances are you're ready for refreshment. **PAM Coffee & Tea Co** (No 2142) offers a vast selection of coffees, teas, ice-creams and muffins amidst a swirl of lilac and sea-green walls. You can go British at **Griffith's** (No 2086) or **Nova Fish & Chips** (No 2209), Greek at **Karas** (No 2024), Tex-Mex at the **Beach Bar** (No 1980), or sample Armenian and Middle Eastern cuisine at **Café Arax** (No 1966).

There's also **Lick's Burgers & Ice Cream** (No 1960), a non-typical selection of pub-style food at **Lion on the Beach** (No 1958), and an international mix of Malaysian, Quebec and Cajun fare amidst old Canadiana surroundings at **Whitlock's** (No 1961).

You can spend endless hours at The Beaches, morning, noon and night. Throughout the summer there's a full program of activities, from Beach fests and children's festivals, to jazz concerts, art exhibitions and walking tours. When you've exhausted your energy, return downtown on the westbound Queen street car.

Option 3. SkyDome

A tour of SkyDome, the world's first multi-purpose stadium with a retractable roof, followed by lunch in the Hard Rock Café or Sightlines Bar.

–To the start: TTC to Union Station, then follow directional signs to the indoor pedestrian walkway that connects Union Station to the SkyDome.–

One-hour tours of **SkyDome** (September to April 10am–4pm; May to June 10am–5pm; July to August 10am–6pm, tel: 341-2770) are offered daily, depending on the event schedule. You don't have to be interested in sports to enjoy the novelty and magnitude of this mega-project.

At the north-east corner of SkyDome, take a moment to savour *The Audience*, 14 large, cartoon-like figures sculpted by Michael Snow. Then purchase your ticket for the tour.

SkyDome has been home to the Toronto Blue Jays baseball team and the Toronto Argonauts football team since 1989. During the early construction stages, in 1986, a team of archaeologists remained on site to examine and rescue valuable finds. As a result, at the beginning of your tour, you pass through an exhibition mounted by the Toronto Historic Board of some of the 1,400 artifacts that were uncovered during the excavation. Besides an assortment of bottles, chinaware and glassware used by Torontonians in the 1800s, significant findings include the remains of **Navy Wharf** (dating back to 1817) and a French cannon built between 1725 and 1750 that was probably used during the War of 1812.

The tour begins with a 15-minute film, *The Inside Story*, which focuses on an illuminating brain-storming session between Roderick Robbie, the architect, and Michael Allen, the engineer, as they tussled with the SkyDome concept. At times their exuberant exchanges seem more philosophical than practical in nature. The actual and awesome mechanics of building the roof, while battling with the elements, are also vividly described by one of the team of construction workers who banged in 250,000 bolts using 2.7-kg (6-lb) sledge hammers.

SkyDome took 2½ years to build, and opened with a Blue Jays game on June 5, 1989. You'll be inundated with facts and trivia as you walk through the various levels, visiting the press box, and a private box along the way. The five levels of seating accommodate 52,000 for baseball games, 53,000 for football matches, and from 10,000 to 70,000 for concerts and other special events. Covering 3.2ha (8 acres), the roof consists of four panels, three of which retract.

Michael Snow's audience

Blue Jays at SkyDome

It glides to an open or shut position at a rate of 21m (71ft) per minute in only 20 minutes. The steel parabolic arches span over 205m (674ft) at the widest point, and are strong enough to bear up to 4.5-m (15-ft) snow drifts.

Described as the world's largest TV screen, **JumboTron** (10m x 33m/33ft x 110ft) is far more than a scoreboard. It takes a full production crew of five cameras and up to 26 people to bring statistics and information on players and teams to the crowd, and within seconds of the action it can rerun plays on the field. At rock concerts (Paul McCartney, Rod Stewart and Elton John have all performed here) and other musical events, JumboTron's close-ups bring the on-stage action closer to the entire audience.

To date, SkyDome's largest crowd – almost 70,000 strong – came to see Hulk Hogan in Wrestlemania. However, 58,000 came to see Genesis, 50,000 filed through the gates to watch the final game when the Blue Jays won the 1992 World Series, and 36,000 turned up to watch the last episode of *Cheers*.

You'll be told some of the hard financial facts behind renting a SkyBox. Corporations have paid a minimum of $1 million for ten years, and that does not include tickets, food or beverages.

At some point along the tour you'll get to sit and gaze out over the 106 rolls of bright green astroturf, held together with 12.8km (8 miles) of zippers, and lit by 776 2,000-watt field lights. Despite the vastness, SkyDome is not intimidating. For all the awesome technology, it's the people on the field, and in the stands, that create SkyDome's magical moments.

After so much excitement – and so many statistics – you'll be ready for lunch. Try the **Hard Rock Café** (besides Gate 1, tel: 341-2389) for an inexpensive lunch surrounded by rock 'n' roll memorabilia, or **Sightlines Bar** (next to the Hard Rock, tel: 341-2381) with an incredible view of the stadium, for a drink and a snack.

Ontario Science Centre appeals to all age groups, and a passion for science is not a prerequisite for an afternoon of enjoyment.

–To the start: easily reached by TTC. Either take Yonge Street subway north to Eglinton station, transfer to the Eglinton East bus and get off at Don Mills Road, or take the Bloor Street subway east to Pape and transfer to the Don Mills bus which stops in front of the Science Centre (770 Don Mills Road). There is plentiful parking if you decide to drive.–

One of the initial goals of the **Ontario Science Centre** (daily 10am–6pm, Friday until 9pm, tel: 696-3127), back in 1964, was that it should be a place of fun and wonder, and should arouse curiosity. By the end of your visit, the chances are you'll agree that this has been achieved. The Centre's three buildings are perched on a steep hillside that plunges down to the **Don River Valley** 27m (90ft) be-

low. They are connected by glassed-in escalators, with glorious views overlooking the wooded ravine.

The main exhibit halls focus on specific themes – communications, space, earth, food, environment, chemistry, sport and technology – and you are encouraged to interact with literally hundreds of the phenomenal exhibits. Follow the signs and descend to **Level C**. On the way, you'll pass the first of several bizarre machines created by British eccentric Rowland Emett, whose whimsical creations combine such everyday items as teaspoons, breadboards, empty wine bottles and decorative lamp shades.

Immediately to your left as you reach Level C is **Exploring Space**. (You should probably arrange when and where to meet up with your companions if you get split up, as it's easy to be diverted.) Amongst many options here, you can experience

Science Centre at exhibit hall

blast-off, a lunar landing and the first steps on the moon through the eyes of an Apollo astronaut. On another computer you can pinpoint an unidentified object flying in space, which will then be identified (most UFOs are debris). Besides the **Star Lab Planetarium** (five shows daily), you can learn about eclipses, the moon, tides and orbits.

In the **Sport** hall, one novel exhibit allows you to do the scoring for an actual winter Olympic sports and then compare your scores with the official judges. You'll find out how the search for a better billiard ball started today's multi-billion dollar plastics industry, and if you're interested in rock climbing, there's an innocuous rock face to be tackled. At the baseball pitching alley there's usually a queue, as would-be pitchers of all ages try to beat the current record for the day or the month.

The final exhibit area on this floor is **Earth and Food**. You can study the mechanics of hydroponics (growing plants in chemical solutions, without soil), digest the history of flour, or mull over a rather graphic exhibit on the human digestive system, including the inside story on parasites – this is not for the squeamish. There's also a direct phone line to the Toronto Weather Office or you can check the latest weather forecasts around the world.

When you're ready, proceed down to **Level D** where **The Living Earth** explores earth's ever-changing ecosystems. There's even a rain forest, complete with a computer-controlled, year-round climate of 28 degrees Celsius (82 degrees Fahrenheit) and almost 100 percent humidity. Four species of endangered poison-dart frogs – safely ensconced in their own climate-controlled homes – live here, as do stick insects, katydids and leaf cutter ants. *A walk in the rain forest*

Throughout the exhibit, the global effects of the destruction of rain forests are all too clearly spelt out.

The inner workings of your own mind, and other people's, are the focus of **Communications**, where you can delve into the living brain, or test your memory by witnessing a crime and then attempting to identify the criminal. You will also find out how easy it is to be duped through auditory illusions and differentiating sounds.

Within **Technology**, you'll come across The Doctor Program, introduced at Massachussets Institute of Technology back in the 1960s, in which you can be 'counselled' by a computer. It has a very interesting response if you decide to get testy! Computers are dotted around throughout the exhibit, and appear to be well used by all visitors whether five or 75 years old.

Aficionados of old cars can test their knowledge on several computer quizzes in **Transportation**, where you can also test your own reaction time in braking. The highlight of the **Science Arcade** is a show on electricity presented by a cheery young technician. In no time at all, children in the audience are clamouring to answer questions. The grand finale – selecting someone from the audience with a long mane to have their hair 'electrified' – is a crowd-pleaser every time. At the Ontario Science Centre the old cliché about time passing quickly when you're having fun proves itself once again.

Island ferry

Option 5. Toronto Islands

A ferry to Centre Island for an afternoon exploring the four main islands – Centre, Ward's, Algonquin and Hanlan's Point – by bicycle, tram, or on foot. Weather and time permitting, stay to enjoy a sunset over downtown Toronto.

–To the start: TTC to Union Station, then take the LRT to the Ferry Terminals at the foot of Bay Street.–

Toronto Islands is a 243-ha (600-acre) park that, centuries ago, was a long sand bar curving westward from Scarborough Bluffs, east of Toronto. It formed a sheltered bay that Colonel Simcoe deemed ideal for a harbour. Thus, the town of York was founded in the early 1790s.

The **Toronto Islands** ferry service (tel: 392-8193) to Ward's Island, Centre Island, and Hanlan's Point runs regularly between 8am and 11.45pm during the summer. Between Labour Day (first Monday in September) and Victoria Day (third Monday in May), the service is limited. Two restaurants and several concession stands operate under the auspices of the Parks Department, summer only, while two cafés on **Ward's Island** are run by local islanders (with somewhat erratic hours). There are also plenty of picnic spots – on beaches, amongst the trees or at the water's edge. (A visit during the winter is an entirely different matter, of course. But if you

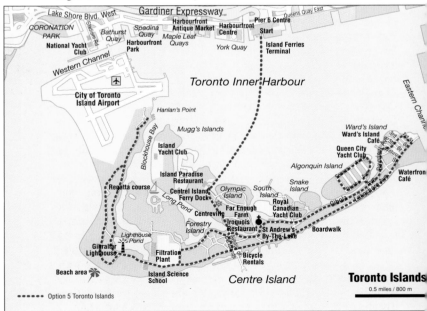

50

rent a pair of ice skates, there can be some divine skating on some of the islands' lagoons.)

The 10-minute ferry ride to Centre Island is one of the best ways to enjoy Toronto's waterfront, busy with water taxis, sail boats, and more commercial traffic. On arrival, follow signs to **Bicycle Rentals**, on the south side of the island. If you prefer walking, the distance from Centre Island Dock to Hanlan's Point is just under 4km (about 2½ miles) and about 2½km (1½ miles) to Ward's Island. A 'trackless train' also regularly circles between the Centre Island Dock and Hanlan's Point.

Bridge over peaceful waters

Severe storms first separated the peninsular from the mainland in 1828. By the mid-19th century, city residents were flocking to the islands to escape the summer heat. Cottages, hotels, an amusement park, even a baseball stadium all sprang up, particularly at Hanlan's Point. **Centre Island** is the most manicured of the group, with its orderly flower beds, fountains and lagoons, and it is always the most crowded.

At the rental shop, you can choose between ordinary bicycles, tandems and two- or four-seater quadricycles. Turn right as you leave the bike rental shop and set off towards **Ward's Island**. The path hugs the shoreline, and soon you will be riding along the somewhat narrower **Boardwalk**. There's no obvious demarcation between Centre Island and Ward's Island but once you come to folksy cottages, you will know you have arrived. The **Waterfront Café** fronts on to the Boardwalk, and may be open.

A cottage community grew up on Ward's and Algonquin islands during the 1920s and 1930s. To this day, the island community is known for its 'alternative' lifestyle, and it has had a long-running battle with city politicians over property ownership. Some islanders are former flower children, but all are committed to island living, year-round. Take time to cycle up and down the narrow streets. Some of the homes have been delightfully spruced up, others, in truth, are somewhat dilapidated. Make your way down to the Ward's Island Ferry Dock, where the nearby **Ward's Island Café** serves an appetizing variety of snacks and drinks, mainly at weekends.

Forever blowing bubbles

Now follow the path on the city side, and head back towards Centre Island. Don't be deterred by the steep bridge over to **Algonquin Island** – it's a worthwhile detour. The streets are named after Indian tribes, a reminder that before the Europeans' arrival, local Indians also regarded the area as a healthy and pleasurable spot to relax.

Return to Ward's and continue your journey, with yacht clubs to your right, parkland to your left. One of Toronto's most prestigious sailing clubs, the **Royal Canadian Yacht Club**, is based here. When the road branches, keep to the right. Soon you will come to **St Andrews-By-The-Lake Church**, built in 1884, the only surviving remnant of the original cottage community.

Go past the bridge to the main Centre Island park, turn right and follow the path beside the water. This stretch is where the Hong Kong Dragon Boat Races take place each summer. Eventually the path curves to the left, and shortly thereafter, joins the trail out to **Hanlan's Point**.

On your left, you'll pass the **Island Science School**, where mainland children get a taste of island living. On the right, beside a stocked trout pond, is **Gibraltar Lighthouse**, built with Queenston limestone in 1806, and Toronto's oldest surviving official building. Detour to the south shore beach for some sunbathing or even swimming (only in August unless you're really hardy) – you'll have it largely to yourself on weekdays. When the road divides, take the left-hand branch, past tennis courts, and the periphery of the airport, to the road's end at Hanlan's Point Ferry Dock.

Hanlan's Point is named after a family that settled here in 1862. One son, Ned Hanlan, later became a world-champion rower. By the 1890s, it was a thriving resort, and in 1910 the aforementioned baseball stadium was built, in which Babe Ruth, a baseball legend, hit his first professional home run. During the 1930s, the stadium closed down, the amusement park was demolished, and construction began on **Toronto Island Airport**. Now the take-offs and landings of small aircraft are the main activity at Hanlan's Point. Follow the left-hand road, past graceful willow trees, picnic benches, and yachts with fanciful names tied up at their moorings. Eventually you'll rejoin the main route, and be on the home stretch to return your bike.

Those of you accompanied by children will unquestionably spend some time at **Centreville** and **Far Enough Farm**. Bumper boat rides, log flume

Royal Yacht Club

Toronto's sparkling skyline

rides, pony rides and a giant ferris wheel are the order of the day, and a guaranteed hit with the junior brigade.

If you didn't bring a picnic, substantial refreshments are available at the **Island Paradise Restaurant**, beside the Centre Island Docks, and the **Iroquois Restaurant** closer to Centreville. For a magical end to the day, find a bench on the city side of the islands, and watch the setting sun cast a warm red glow over downtown Toronto as the lights of the city begin to be switched on. Only then will you be ready to catch the ferry back to the city.

Option 6. Art Gallery of Ontario

The Art Gallery of Ontario owns the world's largest collection of Henry Moore sculptures, and an impressive collection of Inuit and contemporary Canadian art, as well as the works of numerous masters.

Moore's 'Two Forms'

—To the start: TTC to St Patrick subway station.—

Follow directional signs from the subway station and walk west for three short blocks. When you come to Henry Moore's *Two Forms*, at the corner of McCaul Street and Dundas Street West (frequently with one or two youngsters climbing through and around it), you'll have arrived at the **Art Gallery of Ontario** (Wednesday and Friday 10am–10pm, Thursday, Saturday, Sunday and public holidays 10am–5.30pm, tel: 977-0414). If you visit the AGO, as it is commonly called, on a Wednesday afternoon, you will practically have the place all to yourself, because local people are inclined to wait until after 5pm, when admission is free.

The Tanenbaum Atrium

In 1992 the AGO underwent a $58 million expansion that saw the addition of 30 new galleries and the renovation of the 20 existing galleries. Its permanent collection ranges from 15th-century European paintings to international contemporary works of art. Canadian art, including the Inuit works, make up over half the collection. As you roam through the AGO, you'll find that many of the works have been arranged in intimate clusters according to their category, such as Dutch, English Impressionist, Surrealist, or Abstract Expressionist for example.

There's usually a special exhibition just beyond the main entrance, and beyond that, a large area is devoted to 20th-century paintings and sculptures, up to 1960, including works of Auguste Rodin, Amedeo Modigliani, Augustus John, Joan Miró, Marc Chagall and Paul Gauguin. In a small nook off one of the galleries, there's frequently a video playing that's likely to pique your interest, such as, for example, a documentary showing how the weather and light of London affected the paintings of Monet.

The **Joey and Toby Tanenbaum Sculpture Atrium** is a sensational, light-filled, 49-m (160-ft) long, two-storey space which connects the AGO to **The Grange**, a 15-room Georgian mansion built in 1817 that became the first permanent home of the AGO in 1913. Pause for a drink or a snack in the **Atrium Bar** – worth it if only for the chance to take a lingering look at the works of Rodin, David Smith and Michael Snow.

A visit to The Grange is included in your admission fee. Costumed guides enthusiastically explain life in Upper Canada during the 1800s, as you wander from room to room. The building was admirably restored in 1967, and the attention to the smallest detail adds significantly to the fascinating portrayal of everyday life – which was fairly arduous at times, by our standards, even for the upper echelons of Ontario society.

After you re-enter the AGO, you'll come to **A Collector's Cabinet**, an absorbing section based upon the private galleries of European collectors. Ranging from the 16th to 19th century, these galleries were the forerunners of today's museums and galleries. Do look out for Pieter Brueghel the Younger's *Nine Folk Proverbs* – a personal favourite in this area.

The Upper Level of the AGO focuses on 20th-century and contemporary art, Canadian art to 1960 and Inuit art. The international/contemporary works include creations by Mark Rothko (*No 1, White and Red*), Andy Warhol (*Elvis I and II*) and David Hockney (*Lunch at the British Embassy in Tokyo*).

The collection of historical (from the late 18th century) and contemporary Canadian art is outstanding, with a particular emphasis on the work of Toronto and Ontario artists. The Group of Seven (a collection of artists who revolutionized Canadian art in the 1920s) are well represented at the AGO, including works by Tom Thomson, J E H MacDonald, and Lawren S Harris. One room is dedicated to the monumental work of West Coast artist Emily Carr, another to James Wilson Morrice. The warm red walls of **The Salon** are virtually covered with paintings, reflecting the style of 19th-century exhibitions. Other rooms focus on Canada West, Canada East and Upper Canada.

The AGO's Inuit art collection concentrates on work produced since 1948, and includes sculptures, prints, drawings, and a selection of striking wall hangings. Maternal bonding is a recurrent theme, and amongst the collection's highlights are *Mother and Child* by Lucassie Usaitaijuk and *Mother Nursing Child* by John Attok.

One of the absolute highlights of the AGO is the **Henry Moore Sculpture Centre**, which houses the world's largest public collection of this British artist's work. In a coup that most galleries can only dream about, the AGO was the recipient of a substantial part of this collection – including 139 bronzes and original plasters – donated by the sculptor. Moore worked closely with John C Parkin – the architect who designed the Sculpture Centre – and he insisted on overhead natural lighting. Without any doubt, it enhances the primeval feel of Moore's vast human figures, which continue to intrigue and captivate countless AGO visitors.

At the end of your tour, allow time for the newly enlarged **Gallery Shop**, with its wide range of cards, prints, posters and books.

Henry Moore Centre

Ontario Place from the air

Option 7. Ontario Place

A 39-ha (96-acre) waterfront park, Ontario Place is packed with activities for children, but also offers rewarding diversions for unencumbered adults.

—To the start: from Victoria Day (late May) to Labour Day (first Monday in September), a special bus service runs between Union Station and Ontario Place every 15 minutes.—

Call ahead before visiting **Ontario Place** at 955 Lakeshore Boulevard West (Monday to Saturday 10.30am–midnight, Sunday 10.30am–11pm, tel: 314-9900), a seasonal attraction that's open from the latter part of May until early September. Usually admission is free, except for certain attractions. However, there is a charge for concerts, and an overall admission charge during the annual International Fireworks Competition, and the Canadian National Exhibition. A day pass offers unlimited use of all paid attractions except for **bungy jumping** and **parasailing**.

The dazzling white, geodesic dome stands out on the western end of Toronto's waterfront. Designed by Eberhard Zeidler, Ontario Place is three man-made islands connected by a series of bridges. Besides an amphitheatre, a band shell and the Children's Village, a marina accommodates some 300 cruisers and sail boats.

Serious boating

If you have children, you may as well head immediately to the **Children's Village** (although they may try to persuade you to stop at the **Mini Bumper Boats** to your left). From the main entrance, where the bus drops you off, it's a short walk, and you can also rent strollers for a minimal amount.

The Children's Village (admission free) is for the under-12 crowd. Beneath a series of canopies is a wonderful assortment of brightly coloured, soft objects around or through which youngsters can bounce, bump, swing, slide, or crawl. There's also a pre-school section, complete with 'stroller parking'. Nearby, also for under-12s, is a **Waterplay** area, complete with shallow pools, fountains and spouts. Just beyond are the **Waterslide** and the new **Hydrofuge**, a 70 degree slide down which people are hurled and twirled on an eighth of an inch sheet of water. On sweltering days, it keeps children happily and enthusiastically occupied for hours. A little beyond is **Festival Stage**, an open theatre where Polkaroo, the star of a popular television program for children, hosts musical and comedy performances daily.

The Forum is the main reason for Torontonians trekking down to Ontario Place each summer, to listen to its diverse menu of musical offerings, ranging from country to soul, classical to rock. Although there's under-cover seating, on a balmy summer's evening concert-goers are just as happy to hunker down with blankets and cushions upon the grassy banks encircling the stage and be engulfed by the music as the sun sets and the stars appear.

Interconnecting 'pods' built over the water offer more entertainment for the younger visitors. In the **LEGO Creative Play Centre**, there are detailed models of such edifices as St Basil's Cathedral in Moscow, the Eiffel Tower and the Acropolis, as well as numerous play areas, including separate ones for children between 18 months and 3 years. Older children are more likely to head for the **Nintendo Power Pod** or the **3-D Combo-Discovery Theatre**.

Cinesphere, on the westernmost island, is one of the top attractions, for adults at least. The original IMAX movie theatre, it has a gigantic six-storey screen. Wherever you sit, you'll feel part of the action – which can be somewhat disconcerting! A rotation of three dramatic films focusing on subjects that lend themselves to absolutely stunning footage, from underwater to inter-planetary explorations, starts at noon daily.

Cooling off

At the westernmost point of Ontario Place, the six different mazes within **MegaMaze** drive kids crazy and undoubtedly confuse their parents, while everyone has a soakingly good time on the **Wilderness Adventure Ride**.

Although Ontario Place isn't known for its *haute cuisine*, there are plenty of snack bars and full service dining rooms. **Blueberry Hill** in the **West Island Village** is a highly touted hamburger joint, complete with its own bakery. This and several other restaurants overlook **Waterfall Showplace**, where Broadway-style musical revue shows are performed Monday through Saturday on the outdoor stage.

In contrast to the frivolity of most of Ontario Place, a tour of **HMCS Haida**, a World War II destroyer moored near the main entrance, provides an authentic view of shipboard life during the war years.

Option 8. Queen Street West and Environs

A neo-bohemian mecca in downtown Toronto, where the unexpected is the norm, both on the street, and within the boutiques, bistros and book stores of Toronto's trendiest district. There is a wide choice of good restaurants; reservations are recommended for most of them.

—To the start: by TTC to Osgoode station.—

To get the most out of **Queen Street West**, start early in the evening to allow time for browsing before focusing on the evening's activities. As much as anything, people-watching is what makes Queen Street West so much fun. Many of the stores are open till 8pm, some even later. During the warmer months, folk-rock buskers and pavement artists swell the numbers on the sidewalks, as do some panhandlers. Don't be put off by the all-black uniform, shaved heads and pierced appendages of some of the trendier types – many of them students from the nearby Ontario College of Art – it's not *de rigueur*. An evening on Queen Street could be combined with a visit to either the **Royal Alexander Theatre** or the **Princess of Wales** (see *Day 1* for details and *Nightlife* section for phone numbers).

Couture, Toronto-style, is exemplified almost immediately after you set off west from **University Avenue**, along Queen Street, at **Anji Designs** (No 176) and **Fashions by Carlos** (No 176½). **Skin and Bones** (No 180) stocks an excellent selection of North American native arts, crafts and jewellery. If comics are your hobby, here are two comic book stores, **Dragon Lady Comic Shop** (No 200) and one of the biggest in North America, **Silver Snail** (No 367). Caffeine-addicts should know that the **Queen Mother Café** (No 206) features, besides its Laotian/Thai-themed menu, a Caffeine Hour, Monday to Friday, 3–5pm at which large cups of *café au lait* and *cappuccino* replace normal 'Happy Hour' fare.

Queen Street style

Within three short blocks from University Avenue, jazz and classical music buffs should investigate **Second Vinyl** at 2 McCaul Street. Further on, tasty snacks and deliciously refreshing fresh fruit drinks can be bought and enjoyed at the newly renovated **Queen Street Market** (No 238).

The **ChumCity Building** (No 299) is considerably more than a fine example of industrial Gothic architecture, partially adorned with rare terracotta tiles. This former headquarters of the United Church of Canada is now command centre for **CityTV** and **MuchMusic**, two of the hottest TV channels in town. The entire building is wired up as a TV studio, and floor-to-ceiling windows allow passers by to witness live television at any time. On

Street sounds

Black Bull Tavern

Friday evenings, from 9.30–11pm, you can join in **Electric Circus**, a live, inside/outside dance show. Or, 24 hours a day, a one dollar donation to charity will automatically trigger the VideoBox to give you two minutes of airtime on **Speakers Corner**. The wisest, wittiest and zaniest VideoBox contributions are played back every weekend.

Back on the north side of the street, **Express Café** (No 254) dishes up generous bowls of *café au lait*, and a healthy selection of pita bread sandwiches, next door to **Pages Books and Magazines** (No 256). Political correctness is the key here, with a time-absorbing collection ranging from Eastern philosophy to women's studies and cultural theory.

The next block is home to **Venni** (No 274), another local designer, and **Du Verre** (No 280), with its custom-made wrought-iron furniture and hand-blown glass vases. Next door, **Bakka** has a sound reputation as one of the best sci-fi fantasy bookstores in town.

A throng of Harley Davidsons are often parked outside the **Black Bull Tavern** (No 298), while their leather-clad owners quaff ale on the outside patio, but no one is in-

Du Verre designs

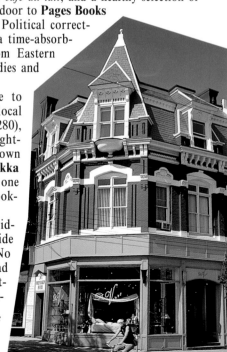

timidated. Beyond **Beverley Street**, the sidewalk on the north side of Queen widens and much of the street theatre takes place over the next few blocks. **Bamboo** (No 312, tel: 593-5771) serves Caribbean and Thai delectables in colourfully exotic surroundings. The cover charge is refunded if you leave before the live act (worldbeat, reggae and African bands play six nights a week) which commences at 10pm – although you will probably want to stay. An eclectic combination of theatre presentations, poetry readings, alternative bands and a pool hall as well as spicy Thai food are guaranteed at **The Rivoli** (No 334, tel: 597-0794), while the superior offerings of the wine bar at **Le Sélect** (No 32, tel: 596-6405) ease the wait for an outside patio table and a chance to sample their delicious *prix fixé*.

As you approach **Spadina Avenue** you'll come to two rather different temples of culture: **Edwards Books & Art**, (No 356) and the **Horseshoe Tavern** (No 370). The Horse-shoe is an institution that has been verging on seedy forever (its dress code states 'Positively no polyester shirts after 10pm'), but it has long been known as a forerunner in presenting talented musicians who have later become some of Canada's best musical acts.

Street stall bargains

Cross Queen Street and walk back along the south side past **Tortilla Flats** (No 429) for Tex-Mex cuisine. At the very least, check out the window of **Fashion Crimes** (No 395), new clothing designed with a vintage look. **Peter Pan** (No 373, tel: 593-0917) is a 1930s-style restaurant with a 1990s menu and a long list of accolades from local food critics. Comforting earth tones and a fireplace sooth diners at **Raclette** (No 361, tel: 593-0934), which specializes in fondues and *raclette* (delicious melted swiss cheese). And there's more French cuisine at **Le Bistingo** (No 349, tel: 598-3490), or Californian at **Soho Bistro** (No 339, tel: 977-3362). Turn right down John Street beside **The Friar & Firkin** (160 John Street), a traditional-style British pub, and enjoy the sensational, up-close view of the CN Tower. If you stinted on dessert earlier, **Just Desserts** (139 John Street) is popular with the after-theatre crowd and anyone else with a sweet tooth.

Italian restaurants are strongly represented along this stretch of John Street, with the **Tuscany Cafe** (tel: 971-4432) on the left and the highly-touted **Orso** (tel: 596-1989) on the right. At King Street West, you can turn right and explore the possibilities of a glass of wine in the cacophonous bar of **Fred's Not Here** (321 King Street West). Or, turn left and head back through the glittering theatre block to the **St Andrew** subway station located at the corner of King and University.

EXCURSIONS

Niagara

A full day, beginning with the 1¼ hour journey to Niagara Falls. There are coach tours from Toronto, but for maximum enjoyment, the trip should be done by car. In Niagara Falls, most attractions are open year round. Although the Shaw Festival in Niagara-on-the-Lake only runs from April to October, there's enough to enjoy in the off-season, particularly for history buffs. Phone ahead for theatre reservations, and book a table for lunch at the Queenston Heights Restaurant.

—To the start: drive to Niagara Falls from Toronto via the Queen Elizabeth Way. Aim to leave by 8am. Follow signs to The Falls. When you reach the Niagara Parkway, turn right and park in the first parking lot with vacancies.—

The formation of the Niagara Escarpment began 450 million years ago when the forces of glacial action compressed ancient mountains into massive layers of rock and culminated in what is now one of the world's top tourist attractions, **Niagara Falls**. There will be no escaping the cloud of spray permanently hovering over the Falls once you join the **Niagara Parkway**, a 56-km (35-mile) route that extends the length of the Niagara River Gorge from Fort Erie to Niagara-on-the-Lake.

As you walk back towards the Falls (if you've ended up far away, the People Mover will transport you up and down the Parkway all day, for the cost of one ticket) look out for the memorial to Father Louis Hennepin, a Belgian missionary who was the chaplain on La Salle's Mississippi expedition in 1679. He supplied the first

Horseshoe Falls, Niagara

Waterproofed tourists

written record we have of the Falls '...there is an incredible cataract or waterfall that has no equal...'.

First-timers to Niagara Falls have no problem identifying with Father Hennepin's awe. As you gaze out from the main viewing deck at **Table Rock House**, over to **Horseshoe Falls**, and the smaller **American Falls**, you can only marvel at the sight of six million cubic feet of water plunging over the Falls every minute.

You may wish to have a quick cup of coffee at the fast food restaurant in Table Rock House. There's usually a lengthy queue for the **Table Rock Scenic Tunnels**. Carved between 1887 and 1902, they lead out to a portal right behind the Falls. However, for a less claustrophobic and truly exhilarating adventure, continue along the Parkway to the complex that serves as base for **Maid of the Mist** (tel: 905-358-5781), actually a fleet of small but sturdy boats that have been venturing into the basin of the Falls since 1846. The trip will supply one of the most lasting memories of your holiday. Be prepared to get wet, despite the protection of the plastic raincoats (supplied). The daunting hubbub of the water as you get closer to the falls is nothing less than awesome.

You'll soon become aware that Niagara Falls ('the honeymoon capital of the world') is full of motels with heart-shaped beds and themed attractions such as **MarineLand**, **Ripley's Believe It or Not**, the **Guinness Book of Records**, **Louis Tussaud's Waxworks**, and more, most of them on **Clifton Hill**. There's no time today, however, to investigate these any further, as you must return to your car.

Drive north up the Niagara Parkway towards **Niagara-on-the-Lake**. Back in 1943, Winston Churchill described the excursion as 'the prettiest Sunday afternoon drive in the world'. From the blossoming of the apple, cherry and peach trees in mid-May to the spectacular displays of fall foliage, it's always a glorious drive through the 1,254 ha (3,099 acres) of immaculate parkland.

The **Niagara River Recreational Trail**, specifically created for pedestrians, joggers and cyclists, also winds its way between the road and the river. There are plenty of parking spots, and if you decide to follow the trail for a while, you're bound to pass some historical markers. The entire area was the scene of fierce and bloody battles during the War of 1812, after the United States first invaded Canada at Queenston, 11km (7 miles) to the north.

Continue along the Parkway, following signs to Queenston Heights, past the **Sir Adam Beck Generating Station**. Although the Niagara River is only 56 km (35 miles) long, it drops a steep 99m (325ft), and its churning waters are one of the world's greatest

Niagara-on-the-Lake

sources of hydro-electric power. The turn-off to **Queenston Heights Park** and **Brock's Monument** is just under a mile past the 15,000-plant **Floral Clock**. The view alone justifies lunch at the **Queenston Heights Restaurant** (tel: 905-262-4274). Perched on the edge of the Niagara Escarpment, the restaurant reigns over an unbeatable view of the lower Niagara River. Reservations are recommended, and the restaurant is closed January through March. A Battle of Queenston Heights walking tour visits every major scene of the pivotal 1812 battle. You may also climb to the top of the 60m (196ft) monument, commemorating General Isaac Brock, the British leader of the Canadian forces killed in the 1812–14 War.

As you continue towards Niagara-on-the-Lake, you enter the heart of Ontario's wine country. Two well-known wineries, **Inniskillin** and **Rief**, have their own boutiques on the Parkway, and offer tours. During the summer, stands selling 'fresh tree-ripened fruit' line the Parkway.

Detour into the village of **Queenston**, site of the invasion by the United States troops in 1812. Canada's only operating Printing Museum can be visited in **Mackenzie House**, where William Lyon Mackenzie first published his strident views on reform in the *Colonial Advocate*, prior to the ill-fated Upper Canada Rebellion in Toronto in 1837.

Back on the Parkway, you'll get frequent glimpses of the river and pass more markers, such as that at **Brown's Point**, where both

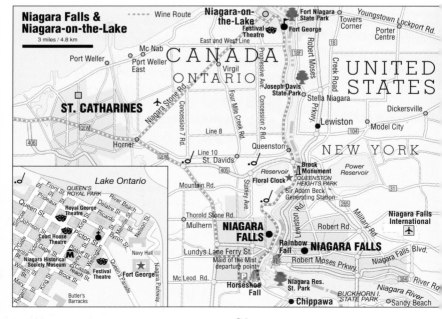

the Canadian York Militia and the American Army bivouacked on separate occasions during the War of 1812. **McFarland House** (open daily during the summer), was built in the early 1800s, and used as a hospital during the war by both British and American forces.

As you enter Niagara-on-the-Lake, **Fort George** (open from late June to October 1) is to your right, a reconstructed fort that was destroyed in 1812. Surrounded by wooden palisades, only the magazine of the original fortress remains, but commentary from costumed guides presents a vivid picture of early 19th-century garrison life.

Niagara-on-the-Lake is a delightful old town, first settled in 1780. The first five sessions of Upper Canada's legislature were held here under Lieutenant Governor John Simcoe, between 1792 and 1796, when the town (then known as Newark) was the capital of Upper Canada. American forces captured it in May 1813, only to burn it down during their withdrawal the following December.

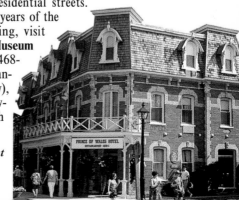

Feast fit for king

The **Shaw Festival Theatre** (tel: 1-800-267-4759) is world-renowned for its production of the works of George Bernard Shaw and his contemporaries. Each year the company presents nine plays in three theatres, the **Festival**, the **Court House** and the **Royal George**.

Park your car – with luck you'll find a space on the main thoroughfare, **Queen Street** – and begin to explore. Practically all the buildings have century-old storefronts. One of the first you'll come to is the **Niagara Apothecary** at 5 Queen Street (May to September, noon–6pm daily) which operated on this site from 1869 to 1960. Now a museum, its black walnut cabinets, rows of antique ceramic storage jars and carefully labelled polished wood drawers show off the accoutrements of a Victorian pharmacy.

Queen Street and adjoining side roads offer shopping enthusiasts an assortment of stores to poke around in, from the long-established **Greaves Jams & Marmalades** (no preservatives, no advertising, non-stop business) to shops selling all kinds of collectibles, plus art galleries, boutiques, cafés, and pubs. Consider eating at one of the local hostelries. You may like the comfortable Victorian elegance of the **Prince of Wales** (6 Picton Street, tel: 905-468-3246) or the dark wood and copper tables of the more informal **Buttery Theatre Restaurant** (19 Queen Street, tel: 905-468-2564).

Wander along the tree-lined residential streets. Most homes were built within 20 years of the town fire in 1813. Time permitting, visit the **Niagara Historical Society Museum** at 43 Castlereagh Street tel: 905-468-3912 (Saturday and Sunday in January and February, otherwise daily), before returning to Toronto, following signs to Highway 55, which joins Queen Elizabeth Way.

Prince of Wales restaurant

Shopping

Toronto has it all. Enormous shopping centres offering every conceivable type of store and service under one roof; residential neighbourhoods where old homes have been converted into specialty stores and boutiques; antique markets and flea markets. From funky second-hand clothing stores to the most elegant of European fashions, from antiquarian books to New Age paraphernalia, the city is a shopper's dream. Most stores are open from 9 or 10am until 6pm, and often later, Monday to Saturday. The shops in the areas described below are all open on Sunday as well, although usually they don't open until noon.

The Eaton Centre

Eaton Centre is a rhapsody to merchandising, with over 350 stores and restaurants spread throughout five levels. It's the flagship location for many of the main fashion chains, such as **Braemar**, **Benetton**, **Gap**, **Jaeger** and **Rodier**, but also houses nifty gift stores such as **Den For Men** and **The Nature Company**. You'll find jewellery and accessories, records and tapes, a variety of specialty shops (**One +**

One Petites and **Silk & Satin**), two banks, a shoe repair outlet, an Ontario Travel Information office, over 50 fast food outlets featuring edibles from around the world, and ten full service restaurants such as **City Grill** with its delightful view and patio overlooking Trinity Square. On the other side of Yonge Street in the **Jewellery Exchange** (295 Yonge Street) you will find more than 60 independent quality jewellers.

Queen's Quay Terminal

Over 100 stores reside in this specialty retail centre at the foot of York Street (see *Day 2*). A very 1990s complex has been created within a historic lakeside building. Contemporary home furnishings, Canadian art and craft, and contemporary fashions for

Eaton Centre

Harbourfront Antique Market

men, women and children all have their place. A few of the many fashion boutiques include **Suitables**, with its classic silk blouses and a discriminating choice of accessories, and **Design Zone**, an exclusive collection of clothing by Canadian designers. Unusual gifts such as decorative art stamps can be purchased at **Great Impressions** while **Mr Music Box** offers an astonishing collection of musical collectibles. Investigate the crafts at **In The Making**, one-of-a-kind leather designs at **Janan Erkan Leather** and hand-painted ceramic ware from Italy at **Muti**. Worth a visit is **Touch The Sky**, for its magical selection of kites, windsocks, windchimes and mobiles. If antiques are your passion, the **Harbourfront Antique Market** is a few minutes walk away, at 390 Queen's Quay West.

Bloor to Yorkville

A large part of the action in Toronto's most elegant shopping zone takes place on and around Bloor Street between Yonge and Avenue Road. It's fun to browse, pricey to shop. There are some exceptions, such as **Science City** in the Holt Renfrew Centre, with

Fashion and fripperies

an amazing assortment of scientific and educational gifts for children and adults. Right on Bloor Street is **Holt Renfrew**, popular with discerning matrons for many years. **Hazelton Lanes Shopping Centre** is possibly the zenith of shopping experiences. Women's and men's fashion boutiques include **Alfred Sung, Chez Catherine, Gianfranco Ferre, Polo/Ralph Lauren**, and **The Original CC Bagg**. Gift stores such as **The Emperor Choice** purvey hand-made *cloisonné* ginger jars while **The Palate** sells quixotic accoutrements for the kitchen. Other specialty stores include **Nanni** in Hazelton Lanes, that sells belts only, **Winston & Homes** on Cumberland Street, with its fine collection of pens, or the Indonesian artifacts and furniture at **Primitives**. Every Toronto bride used to select her fine china from **William Ashley China** which also has the largest Waterford crystal selection outside Ireland. For a superb collection of native and Inuit art, check out **The Guild Shop** on Cumberland. **Louis Wine** on Yorkville specializes in rare 18th-, 19th- and early 20th-century antiques, while **Martin House Dolls** sells collector dolls and bears from all over the world.

Mirvish Village

Mirvish Village and Honest Ed's

It's impossible to miss **Honest Ed's**, at the corner of Bloor and Bathurst (see *Day 3*), with its ostentatious flashing sign of 22,000 light bulbs! Check out – probably briefly – the world-famous bargain shopping centre. People line up to get in, and ten million visit it every year. There's no denying the bargains, and Ed Mirvish ensures that shopping is entertaining as well, through oodles of humorous signs. In considerable contrast, **Mirvish Village** on Markham Street is a small street of tasteful antiques, folk art and vintage clothes stores. There's cinema memorabilia in **Memory Lane** and a world-class book store: **David Mirvish Books on Art**.

Yonge Street, north of Eglinton

Ten minutes by TTC from downtown, get off at Eglinton and walk north. Some would call the area North Toronto, and if you can tear yourself away from the fabulous stores and boutiques, there are some charming, residential side streets with solid older homes and a real sense of family. But first, the stores! For fashion stores with a unique stock, head to **The Casual Way**, **Evviva**, **Mendocino**, **Venni**, and **Higher Ground** (one for adults, one for children). For gifts with a difference, the choice is wide – **UnderWraps**, **The Little Party Shoppe**, **SendSations**, **Seaforth**, and **La Cache**. There are two shops devoted to Western regalia, almost side by side – **Bootmaster** and **Bow Valley Boot Company**. Canadian designers are behind the colourful, funky clothing for kids at **Crazy Mommas**, while unexpected treasures are to be found at **The Poke-About**. **Sporting Life** is mecca for the Toronto area sporty crowd. When they have a sale, parking is impossible. There are new and rare books at **Contact Editions**, excellent reading at the Children's Bookstore, gourmet cookies at **Monsieur Félix & Mr Norton**, and mouth-watering pastries and coffee at **Pyramid Cakery**.

Queen Street West

This has already been covered in *Pick & Mix Option 8*. If you decide to make it a daytime outing, you will find all the stores mentioned there, along with others such as **The Allery** for antique prints and maps; and silks, cottons and linens at **Ms Emma Designs**.

Eating Out

Deciding where to eat in Toronto can be an oner-
ous task, with over 4,000 restaurants to choose from. The waves
of immigrants that have arrived in the city over the last hundred
years from all parts of the globe have had a dramatic impact on
the eating habits of the most WASP (an acronym for White Anglo-
Saxon Protestant) of Torontonians.

There are few restaurants that specialize purely
in Canadian cuisine, although Metropolis at
838 Yonge Street is one, but a wide range
of traditional Canadian foodstuffs and
dishes make frequent appearances on
menus – from Atlantic or BC salmon to
fiddleheads from New Brunswick, from
Quebec tortière to Canadian back bacon.
And some of the excellent Canadian wines
that have been acquiring top prizes at numerous international wine competitions are now
appearing on the wine list.

Stop for a snack

Besides the cuisines of the restaurants listed below,
Torontonians can select from Argentinian, Armenian, Czechoslo-
vakian, Danish, Estonian, Ethiopian, Hungarian, Korean, Kosher,
Mexican, Persian, Filipino, Somalienne, or Sri Lankan fare – and
much more besides!

The art of eating has risen to such heights that certain chefs,
such as Greg Couillard, Jamie Kennedy and Mark McEwan, are
followed faithfully from restaurant to restaurant. Other diners pay
homage to restaurant owners such as Franco Prevedello and Michael
Carlevale, who between them have brought into being some of the
best Italian restaurants in the city – and Toronto has no shortage
of excellent Italian restaurants.

The peak dining hour varies from restaurant to restaurant. It is
best to check by phone first if you like to dine with the crowd, but
want to be sure that you can guarantee a table. Reservations in advance are always ad-
visable for the higher priced
restaurants. An approximate price
guideline per person, excluding alcohol, taxes and tips is as follows:
$ = under $20; $$ = under $30;
$$$ = under $40.

Street eating

American

ALICE FAZOOLI'S
294 Adelaide Street West
Tel: 979-1910
A boisterous atmosphere in a former printing plant. The menu ranges from Cajun, Italian and Thai to good ol' American steaks. Huge portions match the size of the place. **$$**

FRED'S NOT HERE
321 King Street West
Tel: 971-9155
Verging on raucous, especially downstairs in The Red Tomato. Wacky decor and an imaginative menu. Thai High Prawn soup gives a new meaning to 'red hot lips' but it is really delicious. **$$**

Jamaican hot spot

CAFÉ LA GAFFE
24 Baldwin Street
Tel: 596-2397
A wide-ranging menu from many countries adapted to Californian cuisine and a convivial meeting place for the more cerebral crowd. **$$**

SOUTHERN ACCENT
595 Markham Street
Tel: 536-3211
Good Southern vittles such as blackened chicken livers, Cajun gumbo and zydeco greens served by hip young serving staff in a renovated two-storey Victorian house. **$$**

Asian

BANGKOK GARDENS
18 Elm Street
Tel: 977-6748
Spicey Thai noodles served amidst a teak decor, complete with waterfall. Star dish is the Royal Barge. **$$**

OLE MALACCA
49 Baldwin Street
Tel: 340-1208
Traditional Malaysian dishes redolent with chili, curry and garlic. Heaven at the right price. **$**

Caribbean

THE REAL JERK
709 Queen Street East
Tel: 463-6906
Reggae pounds away at this Jamaican hot spot. Goat curry and chicken roti are the best bets. **$**

Chinese

CHAMPION HOUSE
478 Dundas Street W
Tel: 977-8282
A popular haunt which some believe serve the perfect Peking Duck. Must be ordered in advance. **$$**

LEE GARDEN
331 Spadina Avenue
Tel: 593-9524
Superb Cantonese dishes (check the daily specials) served amidst lots of hullabaloo. A popular eatery with the locals in Chinatown. **$**

NEW GRAND SEAFOOD HOUSE
615 Gerrard Street East
Tel: 778-8888
Try *dim-sum* for Sunday brunch, when the place is hopping with Chinese families. Ever-circulating servers dispense delicacies from their trollies. **$**

Ripe and juicy peaches

Continental

DA DANTE
3353 Yonge Street
Tel: 486-2288
Worth the trek up Yonge Street to this fine eatery. Home-cooking, Italian-style, in sunny surroundings. $$

EPISODE
195 Carlton Street
Tel: 921-1255
An exotic mixture of European and Asian influences at this intimate restaurant in Cabbagetown. $$$

THE ROSEDALE DINER
1164 Yonge Street
Tel: 923-3122
A cosy space where food ranges from fresh salmon cakes and Rosedale burgers to Mediterranean or Californian entrées, and scrumptious desserts. $$

Eclectic

GROWLERS
75 Victoria Street
Tel: 360-5877
Mexican, Cajun and Italian fare is served in the downstairs bar of this micro-brewery. Growler's Pizza is an excellent choice. Generous helpings for unbeatable value. $

MACCHERONI
81 Bloor Street East
Tel: 515-7560
Dazzling decor and chipper service; mostly Italian fare. $

French

BISTRO 990
990 Bay Street
Tel: 921-9990
Beloved bistro where French provincial fare is served in a farmhouse setting. Next best thing to a holiday. $$$

BROWNES BISTRO
4 Woodlawn Avenue East
Tel: 924-8132
Another Rosedale eatery, owned by a former Cordon Bleu teacher. Delectable offerings in a tranquil ambience that is, quite simply, French. $$

Greek

PHILOXENIA
519 Danforth Avenue
Tel: 461-1997
One of the quieter Greek restaurants along Danforth, but the flavours and aromas are the real thing. Possibly the best lamb *souvlaki* in town. $$

Indian

INDIAN RICE FACTORY
414 Dupont Street
Tel: 961-3472
A little off the beaten track, but a worthwhile detour. Fresh, succulent ingredients and sizzling spices. $

MOGHUL DOWNTOWN
33 Elm Street
Tel: 597-0522
Northern Indian cooking, specializes in vegetarian and tandoori. $$

The splendid Splendido

Italian

SPLENDIDO
88 Harbord Street
Tel: 929-7788
Colourful and zany decor, it's a place to be seen as well. Grilled sea bass and chicken roasted in a wood burning oven are two of its specialties. $$$

CENTRO
2472 Yonge Street
Tel: 483-2211
Northern Italian cooking amidst art deco surroundings. Expensive but quite unmissable; the downstairs wine and pasta bar is more affordable. $$$

ENOTECA
150 Bloor Street West
Tel: 920-9900
Connected to the far pricier Prego della Piazza, Enoteca features a stylish assortment of pizza and lighter dishes. Delightful outside patio. $$

Japanese

MADOKA
252 Dupont Street
Tel: 924-3548
A traditionally serene dining room with a wide range of *sushi* and charming service. $$

Middle Eastern

BYZANTIUM
499 Church Street
Tel: 922-3859
Relax over their exotically flavoured martinis before getting into the Middle Eastern dips. Some delectable hot appetizers – the Persian spiced chicken is utterly divine. $$

KENSINGTON KITCHEN
124 Harbord Street
Tel: 961-3404
Sone of the best, and cheapest, Middle Eastern food in town. $

Waiting for customers

Seafood

BY-THE-BRIDGE
52 St Clair Avenue East
Tel: 964-2288
Impressively extensive menu at this action-packed venue. $$

PHEBE'S
641 Mount Pleasant
Tel: 484-6428
Imaginative specials, and the mussels are out of this world. $$

RODNEY'S OYSTER HOUSE
209 Adelaide Street East
Tel: 363-8105
A tiny restaurant, only five tables plus seating at the bar. Reservations taken for three or more. Oysters and mussels served with lip-searing sauces. $$

Nightlife

With over 140 theatre and dance companies, Toronto has the third-largest theatre industry in the English-speaking world, after London and New York. Besides blockbusters such as *Miss Saigon* and *Phantom of the Opera,* theatre productions range from the traditional to the alternative.

Excellent Canadian works are produced by the Tarragon Theatre, Theatre Passe Muraille and Factory Theatre, while there's fun but thought-provoking theatre for children at Young People's Theatre. Buddies in Bad Times focuses largely, but not entirely, on gay and lesbian issues. Same day, half-price tickets for theatre and dance events can be purchased at the TO TIX booth (tel: 596-8211), at the corner of Yonge and Dundas, just outside the Eaton Centre (Tuesday to Saturday noon–7.30pm, Sunday 11am–3pm).

Music also flourishes: the Toronto Symphony Orchestra performs almost 10 months a year in the Roy Thomson Hall, while the illustrious productions of the Canadian Opera Company and the National Ballet of Canada draw audiences to the O'Keefe Centre year after year. The Glenn Gould Studio, based in the Canadian Broadcasting Corporation headquarters, is a combined recording studio and public concert hall, designed principally for classical and jazz music. The Recital Hall, in the new North York Centre for the Performing Arts, recently opened to ecstatic reviews.

Other options include a Tafelmusik concert – a Toronto-based, internationally-acclaimed orchestra specializing in baroque music – or one of the regular poetry readings at the Idler pub.

Although Toronto's clubs are spread across the city, there are plenty of places to shimmy, line dance, or simply rock, for those so inclined.

For comprehensive listings on all performances and events, check either *Now* or *Eye*, free weekly newspapers available in many restaurants. Tickets for most events, including sporting events, can be purchased through Ticketmaster (tel: 872-1111) using a credit card. A service charge of from $2 to $5 is added to the ticket price, depending on the event.

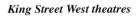

King Street West theatres

Skating at City Hall

PRINCESS OF WALES THEATRE
300 King Street West
Tel: 872-1212

ROYAL ALEXANDRA THEATRE
260 King Street West
Tel: 872-3333

Music

GLENN GOULD STUDIO
250 Front Street W
Tel: 205-5555

MASSEY HALL
178 Victoria Street
Tel: 593-4828

NORTH YORK PERFORMING ARTS CENTRE
5040 Yonge Street
Tel: 324-5800

O'KEEFE CENTRE
1 Front Street
Tel: 872-2262

ROY THOMSON HALL
60 Simcoe Street
Tel: 593-4828

Dance

PREMIERE DANCE THEATRE
207 Queens Quay West
Tel: 973-4000

Theatre

BUDDIES IN BAD TIMES THEATRE
142 George Street
Tel: 863-9455

CANADIAN STAGE COMPANY
27 Front Street East
Tel: 368-3110

FACTORY THEATRE
125 Bathurst Street
Tel: 864-9971

PANTAGES THEATRE
263 Yonge Street
Tel: 872-2222

TARRAGON THEATRE
30 Bridgman Avenue
Tel: 531-1827

THEATRE PASSE MURAILLE
16 Ryerson Avenue
Tel: 363-2416

Pubs, Clubs and Lounges

AQUARIUS 51 LOUNGE
55 Bloor Street West
Tel: 967-5225
The highest piano lounge in the city, on the 51st floor of the ManuLife Centre, this is the perfect spot for a romantic tryst.

BIG BOP
651 Queen Street West
Tel: 366-6699
Classic '60s and '70s on one floor, '80s and '90s party music on another, alternative on the top floor.

BLACK SWAN
154 Danforth Avenue
Tel: 469-0537
Great blues sessions on Wednesday evenings and Saturday afternoons.

BOVINE SEX CLUB
542 Queen Street West
Tel: 367-4239
Plays both rock 'n' roll and alternative music.

BRUNSWICK HOUSE
481 Bloor Street West
Tel: 924-2242
A long-time favourite hang-out with the university crowds. Some of the top blues bands play in **Albert's Hall** upstairs.

C'EST WHAT
67 Front Street East
Tel: 867-9499
Just about everything plays here – folk, R&B, country, jazz, pop, dance and rock artists.

CHICK 'N' DELI
744 Mount Pleasant Road
Tel: 489-3363
A neighbourhood bar with great ambience and cheap food, as well as good live jazz and R&B.

DUKE OF WESTMINSTER
First Canadian Place
Tel: 368-1555
Oak-panelled, British-style pub in the heart of Toronto's financial district.

EL MOCAMBO
464 Spadina Avenue
Tel: 922-1570
A fixture on the scene – the Rolling Stones played here in the '70s – and it's still going strong.

GEORGE'S SPAGHETTI HOUSE
290 Dundas Street East
Tel: 923-9887
Longest running jazz club in the city. Moe Koffman performs one week a month, for which you need to book.

KLUB MAX
52 Peter Street
Tel: 597-1567
Three clubs for the 19–30 crowd: alternative in the basement, dance on the first floor, rock on the second. All-night party every Saturday.

A bite with a beat

LEE'S PALACE
529 Bloor Street West
Tel: 532-7632
A popular alternative rock band venue in the University of Toronto neighbourhood.

LOOSE MOOSE TAP & GRILL
220 Adelaide Street West
Tel: 971-5252
The decor's a fun spoof on Canada's North. Rock 'n' roll from the '60s to the '90s keeps the crowds hopping.

MADISON
14 Madison
Tel: 927-1722
A popular watering hole with students and the Anglo/Irish crowd.

McVEIGH'S NEW WINDSOR TAVERN
124 Church Street
Tel: 364-9698
An Irish-owned pub where the Celtic atmosphere is the real thing.

MONTREAL RESTAURANT/BISTRO JAZZ CLUB
65 Sherbourne Street
Tel: 363-0179
Three sets nightly of modern, New Orleans and traditional jazz in an intimate speak-easy atmosphere.

Outdoor nightlife

PHOENIX CONCERT THEATRE
410 Sherbourne Street
Tel: 323-1251
Two huge dance rooms: DJs play rock, alternative, rock 'n' roll and disco.

RPM
132 Queen's Quay East
Tel: 869-1462
A long-established mega-club: '80s dance music, disco, live rock 'n' roll.

THE NEW GASWORKS
585 Yonge Street
Tel: 922-9367
One of Toronto's oldest rock 'n' roll venues, recently revived.

THE SALOON
901 King Street West
Tel: 360-1818
Huge country bar. Big-name entertainers, packed dance floor.

SECOND CITY
110 Lombard Street
Tel: 863-1111
Live revue comedy and theatre. Dinner/theatre packages available.

TOP O' THE SENATOR
253 Victoria Street
Tel: 364-7517
Live jazz above diner-style restaurant.

YUK YUK'S
1280 Bay Street
Tel: 967-6425
Stand-up comedy nightly. Dinner/show packages available.

Gay Scene

BADLANDS
9 Isabella Street
Tel: 960-1200
Country and western rules. Regular classes in Beginner's Line Dancing and Two-Step Instruction.

EL CONVENTO RICO
750 College Street
Tel: 588-7800
Latin club for gays and lesbians.

THE ROSE CAFÉ
547 Parliament Street
Tel: 928-1495
A popular lesbian bar, with pool tables, a games room, a country and western/rock 'n' roll dance bar and a mainly vegetarian restaurant.

TRAX
529 Yonge Street
Tel: 963-5196
A long-established, very popular gay club with six different bars to choose from, including a piano bar, a dance bar and a games room.

Calendar of Special Events

All public holidays are marked with an asterisk.

JANUARY / FEBRUARY

New Year's Day*
Toronto International Boat Show (early January): attracts serious and wanna-be nautical enthusiasts.

Toronto International Auto Show (mid-January): the latest in automotive trends and technology.

MARCH / APRIL

Toronto Sportsmen's Show (mid-March): targets the huntin' and fishin' brigade.

One of a Kind Craft Show (end of March, beginning of April): a vast range of uniquely handcrafted articles are displayed.

A Blue Jay hero

Good Friday* and **Easter Sunday*** (end of March, beginning of April)

Toronto Blue Jays take up residence at SkyDome for the upcoming American League baseball season.

MAY

International Children's Festival (mid-May): performers from around the world including mime artists and jugglers.

Shoppers Drug Mart Marathon (mid-May): thousands of runners participate in this annual event in downtown Toronto.

Victoria Day* (fourth Monday in May)

JUNE

Metro Toronto International Caravan (mid-June): a week-long celebration during which the cuisine and culture of Toronto's ethnic communities are experienced in over 40 pavilions.

Du Maurier Ltd Downtown Jazz (last week): a 10-day festival featuring over 500 Canadian and international musicians at free daily concerts as well as at ticketed galas and on jazz cruises.

Benson & Hedges Symphony of Fire (end of June, beginning of July): nu-

merous countries compete in a spectacular fireworks competition that lights up the sky above Ontario Place.

Dragon Boat Race Festival (mid-June): a well-attended event on Toronto Islands that successfully reproduces the excitement of its namesake in Hong Kong.

Queen's Plate (last Saturday): the oldest stakes race in North America, held at the Woodbine Race Track.

JULY

Canada Day* (July 1): day-long celebrations with special events at Harbourfront Centre and Nathan Phillips Square.

CHIN Radio Station Picnic (first weekend): sponsored by the local Italian radio station, it's a gigantic, three day funfest on Toronto Island.

Beaches Jazz Festival

Fringe of Toronto Festival (first 10 days): avant-garde works are performed throughout the Annex neighbourhood by almost 80 theatrical companies and over 400 performers from around the world.

Beaches International Jazz Festival (last weekend): an annual musical gathering in the Kew Gardens Bandshell, and along Queen Street East from Woodbine to Beech.

Molson Indy (middle weekend): attracts the world's racing super-stars.

Toronto Outdoor Art Exhibition (mid-July): an annual art festival that features works by artists from across Canada, the United States and Europe. **Caribana** (last week): a Mardi Gras-like 10-day celebration of the lively West Indian spirit, highlighted by a parade of 5,000 celebrants in dazzling costumes.

AUGUST

Civic Holiday* (first Monday)

Canadian National Exhibition (mid-August to Labour Day weekend): The world's largest, and oldest annual fair: exhibitions, grandstand shows, a midway and an air show.

Celebrating Caribana

Flying high at CNE

SEPTEMBER

Labour Day* (first Monday)

Cabbagetown Festival (second weekend): tours of homes and gardens, a film festival and a parade in one of Toronto's oldest neighbourhoods.

Festival of Festivals (second week): the second-largest film festival in the world. Stars and cinematographers get together to celebrate the world of cinema.

Artsweek '93 (last week): an annual celebration of art in Toronto, including behind-the-scenes tours of theatres and studios.

The Word On The Street (last Sunday): crowds jam Queen Street West during this annual book and magazine fair and authors read from their new fall titles.

Canadian Open Golf Championship: an end-of-summer high point for golf enthusiasts.

OCTOBER

Thanksgiving Day* (second Monday)

International Festival of Authors (middle week): a major cultural event. Writers from around the globe give nightly readings from their work, at Harbourfront Centre.

NOVEMBER

One of a Kind Craft Show (end of November/beginning of December): a 10-day opportunity to buy some rare

Christmas gifts from over 500 craftspeople and artists from across Canada.

Royal Agricultural Winter Fair (mid-November): the world's largest indoor fair. Also includes the Royal Horse Show, the highlight of Canada's equestrian season. The fair is a 10-day event focusing on food, animals (over 10,000 of them), exhibitions and competitions.

Christmas Past in Historic Houses (mid-November to mid-January): three

Royal Agricultural Fair

of the historical homes owned by the Toronto Historical Board, Colborne Lodge, Mackenzie House and Spadina, recreate a Dickens, Victorian and Edwardian Christmas respectively.

Cavalcade of Lights (last Friday): a family affair, as the city's Christmas lights are switched on by the mayor, and professional ice skaters thrill the crowds in Nathan Phillips Square.

DECEMBER

Christmas Day* (25th)

Boxing Day* (26th)

New Year's Eve* (31st): alcohol-free celebrations in Nathan Phillips Square and other downtown locations, including many of the theatres have become a popular family outing.

PRACTICAL information

Telephone numbers for the Toronto area are mostly within area code 416. An area code will only be shown if it is different. The 1-800 numbers are toll-free if the calls are made within Canada.

Pearson International Terminal

GETTING THERE

By Air

Toronto's Lester B Pearson International Airport is on the northwest corner of Metro Toronto, 32km (18 miles) from the downtown core. With the 1991 opening of the privately owned and operated Terminal 3, the airport is now linked by over 35 airlines to major American and international destinations. (Plans are currently in the works for Terminals 1 and 2 to be taken over by private enterprise on a 50-year lease.) Pacific Western provides an Airport Express bus service (tel: 672-0293) every 20 minutes from all three terminals to several downtown hotels (approximately $11 one way, $20 round trip) as well as to three subway stations, Islington, Yorkdale and York Mills. The service operates between 4.30am and 12.35am. The journey takes approximately 40 minutes. There are separate taxi and limousine stands at the arrivals level of each terminal. Only taxis with TIA on their license plates are authorized to pick up passengers from Pearson International Airport, and the fare to the centre of the city is approximately $35. The limousine services, with their larger cars and uniformed drivers, charge a set fee, which is usually in the $35-$40 range.

Toronto is also served by the Toronto Island Airport, which handles short-haul commuter flights. Located in the main harbour area, it's a brief ferry ride to the foot of Bathurst Street, and a very short taxi ride to the downtown core.

By Rail

VIA **Rail** and **Amtrak** both operate passenger rail service from Union Station, connecting Toronto to cities across Canada and within the United States. Although there is not much cost difference between train and air tickets (depending on the season, or the day of the week), rail travel offers a more relaxed way of viewing the countryside, and the train deposits you right in the heart of Toronto. For information about train travel with either company, tel: 366-8411.

By Road

If you are driving up from New York State, the Queen Elizabeth Way is the main highway between New York State and Toronto. Highway 401, on the northern edge of the city, extends from Windsor (3 hours) and Michigan in the west, to Montreal (5½ hours) in the east (once within Quebec, it becomes Highway 20). Highway 401 is North America's second busiest highway, with first place going to the San Diego Freeway. As a result, the police strictly enforce the speed limit on various sections of the highway. Signs for distances and speed limits are shown in kilometres, with the speed limit of 100km/h (60mph) on highways, 60km/h (35mph) in the city. None of the aforementioned highways are particularly scenic, but they are fast, and there are numerous fast food restaurants and gas stations with attractive picnic areas behind in which to stretch your legs. Note that the use of seat belts is mandatory in Ontario, under provincial law.

By Bus

The main bus terminal is at 610 Bay Street, at the corner of Bay and Dundas Streets, very close to City Hall and Eaton Centre. It is the base for Greyhound Lines of Canada (tel: 594-0343), a national company that offers scheduled services from across the country and links into the Greyhound system within the United States, and several other bus companies.

TRAVEL ESSENTIALS

Visas & Passports

Foreign visitors from countries other than the United States must have a valid passport to enter Canada. US citizens and legal residents don't need passports or visas (although they are preferred). Native born US citizens should have a birth or voter's certificate, naturalized American citizens need naturalization certificates or other evidence of citizenship, and permanent residents who are not citizens must have their alien-registration receipt. If a stay of over three months is planned, for any nationality, a visa may be required.

Customs

Visitors from America or overseas who are at least 19 years old are allowed to bring in 1.4 litre (40oz) of liquor or wine, up to 12 bottles or cans (355ml/12oz each) of beer, and gifts not exceeding $60. Duty and tax has to be paid on the balance if the gifts are worth over $60. Anyone over 16 years old may bring in 200 cigarettes, 400gms (14oz) of tobacco and 50 cigars. There are also restrictions on importing meats, dairy products and agricultural products. A rabies certificate has to be presented by the owners if a pet is brought into Canada.

Winter transport

Weather

Toronto's location on the north shore of Lake Ontario ensures a reasonably temperate climate, particularly compared with the rest of Ontario, which suffers considerably harsher winters. The lake acts as a coolant during the summer, yet keeps the city warmer during the winter. Summers are fairly dry and warm (average temperature: +23°C/73°F), winters are cool with a minimum of snow (-6°/21°F). Spring (+6°C/42°F) and fall (+10°C/50°F) can be most pleasant, with sunny days and cooler nights. For an up-to-date forecast on weather in the Toronto area, tel: 676-3066. For out-of-town weather, tel: 676-4567.

Clothing

Much depends on the time of year you plan to visit. If you come during the winter, heavy warm coats and boots are essential. Being a cosmopolitan city, very little raises eyebrows these days. However,

Ready to glide

population. In 1989 the United Nations deemed it the world's most ethnically diverse city. The influence of the immigrants and refugees on Toronto, over the years, has created a vibrant, cosmopolitan city.

MONEY MATTERS

Although there is no limit to the amount of money a visitor can bring into Canada, technology in the banking field has virtually eradicated the need to bring in huge sums. Any bank or exchange house can change foreign currency for Canadian funds, and many stores, hotels and restaurants accept American currency. Most downtown banks are open from either 8am–4pm or 9am–5pm, and there are cash machines on almost every corner. Major credit cards are also accepted at most establishments. If you bring traveller's cheques, the transaction is simplest if they are in Canadian funds. The exchange rate compared with the US dollar has made Canada a tremendous bargain for American visitors recently, and has alleviated, to an extent, the effect of our taxes.

Taxes

Welcome to the land of confusion. A provincial sales tax of 8 percent is levied on goods and services. Visitors can apply for a refund provided they have accumulated over $100 worth of receipts for non-disposable merchandise to be used outside Ontario. For information on this refund, as well as for a refund of the 5 percent accommodation sales tax that is charged by all hotels, tel: 314-0944, 314-0956 (English); 1-800-268-3736 (French); 1-800-268-3735 (Canada and Continental US, except Yukon and Northwest Territories).

The Goods and Services Tax (GST) of 7 percent is charged on most goods and services sold in Canada. Visitors can claim a rebate of the GST paid on short-term accommodation of less than a month, and on most goods they bought to take home. Your rebate has to be at least $7 and goods have to have been purchased no more than one year ago. For information on getting the rebate, tel: 1-800-668-4748 from anywhere in Canada, or 613-991-3346 from outside Canada.

since walking is one of the best ways to get to know the city, bring comfortable footwear. During the daytime, casual wear is perfectly acceptable. If some of your evening activities are likely to include concert-going or dining at some of Toronto's smarter restaurants, more formal dress would be appropriate. During the heat of the summer, when most buildings are air-conditioned, it's a good idea to have a light jacket or sweater to put on, as you can cool down very quickly. Likewise, during the winter months, buildings are kept extremely warm (by British and European standards, at least) and it is not necessary to wear layers of thick sweaters – unless you like to roast!

Electricity

Standard 110 Voltage is used in Canada, the same system as in the United States. Visitors from the US do not need to bring electrical adapters or converters.

GETTING ACQUAINTED

Geography and Population

Toronto is on the northern shore of Lake Ontario, 558km (349 miles) west of Montreal, 131km (81 miles) from Niagara Falls, Ontario, 154km (95 miles) from Buffalo, New York and 378km (235 miles) from the Windsor/Detroit area. Between road, rail, water (through the Port of Toronto) and air, the city is well-connected to all parts of the province, the continent and the world.

One of Toronto's charms is that despite being one of the world's fastest growing cities, it still has a much treasured system of ravines that criss-cross the city, providing a wilderness of sorts for the 3.8 million people who inhabit the Greater Metropolitan Toronto area. Indeed, Toronto is the largest city in Canada, with 14 percent of the country's 26 million

Tipping

In restaurants the service charge is rarely included in the bill and the usual tip is 15 percent. Still under discussion since the introduction of the GST is whether the tip should be on the total of the bill, or on the pre-tax total. The final decision rests with the customer, and often depends on the size of the bill. Taxis and limousine drivers are usually given a 10 percent to 15 percent tip, hotel porters expect at least 50 cents per bag and room service is $1 per day per person. Tips in American currency are always particularly and gratefully received.

Bilingual signpost

GETTING AROUND

Public Transit

The Toronto Transit System (TTC) is an excellent public transit system, that is clean, safe and inexpensive. Its underground subway trains connect with aboveground buses and street cars to provide a vast network right across the city. A transfer ticket enables you to switch from the subway to a bus or street car and there is a considerable saving if you buy 10 at a time. There are also two Day Passes, each priced at approximately $5. The first is good for one person, for unlimited travel after 9.30am, Monday to Saturday. The second – and this is an amazing bargain – is for up to two adults and four children on Sundays and holidays. There are two main lines – a U-shaped

Trolley in a hurry

north–.south line and one east–west line, with an extension from Union Station down to Harbourfront via the Harbourfront LRT. For full details on fares and routes, pick up the Ride Guide from the subway collectors' booths, or call TTC Information, tel: 393-4636 (7am–10pm daily). **GO Transit** operates a regular bus and train service that connects suburban areas, some fairly far afield, to various TTC stations and downtown Toronto.

Car Rental

Driving a car around Toronto is fairly straightforward provided you have a good map that marks the one-way streets. However, parking lots are fairly expensive, especially during the day, and street parking can be difficult to find. The major car rental companies are located at the airport, and have offices downtown. Some of the main companies are:

Alamo Rent A Car tel: 1-800-327-9633
Avis Rent A Car tel: 1-800-879-2847
Budget Rent A Car tel: 1-800-268-8900
Discount Car and Truck Rentals tel: 1-800-263-2355
Dollar Rent A Car tel: 1-800-800-4000
Hertz tel: 1-800-263-0600
Thrifty Car Rental tel: 1-800-367-2277
Tilden Interrent tel: 922-2000/different 800 numbers, depending on area of origin of the call.

Tours

There are several special interest tours available, although not all of them are operated year-round.

Toronto Harbour and Islands Boat Tours tel: 364-2412
David Ko's Chinatown Walking Tour tel: 599-6855
Toronto Architecture Tour tel: 922-7606
Toronto Historical Board's Walking Tours tel: 392-6827

Taxis

Except in the middle of a snow storm, it is usually easy to hail a cab, certainly in the downtown area. There are also taxi stands outside the main hotels, Union Station, and dotted throughout the financial core of the city. Drivers are not allowed to pick up two fares unless a customer advises the driver to pick up the second one. The largest taxi companies:
Beck Taxi tel: 449-6911
Co-op Cabs tel: 364-8161
Diamond tel: 366-6868
Metro Cab tel: 363-5611
Sunnyside Taxi tel: 535-1121

Underground City

There's practically a separate city underneath downtown – a 10km (6 mile) network known as PATH, which extends six blocks north from Front Street to Dundas Street and five blocks west, from Yonge Street over to John Street. It can be entered from any of the downtown subway stations, several of the main hotels and many of the larger office complexes. The shops below ground are as varied as the ones above, and during any extremes of climate – hot or cold – the Underground City provides instant succour.

HOURS AND HOLIDAYS

Business Hours

Most offices are open from 9am–5pm, although as flexi-hour work schedules gain in popularity, many open earlier. Government offices are usually open from 8.30am–5pm, and the main downtown Post Office at 36 Adelaide Street East is open 8am–5.45pm, Monday to Friday. Opening hours of stores have changed tremendously over the last couple of years, particularly since Sunday opening has been allowed. The main downtown stores open at 10am (although closing hours vary from 6pm to 9pm Monday to Friday). Weekend hours are usually Saturday 9am–9pm, Sunday noon–5pm. Eaton Centre is open Monday to Friday 10am–9pm, Saturday 9am–9pm, Sunday noon–5pm.

Public Holidays

See *Calendar of Events*.

ACCOMMODATION

Since most of the tours suggested in this book are in and around downtown Toronto, the hotels recommended are all in the downtown area. Fortunately, there is accommodation to match every budget. Although the rates quoted are for the lowest rack rate for a standard double room, do enquire about special packages and promotions when making reservations. All hotel accommodations are subject to 5 percent sales tax and 7 percent Goods & Services Tax. (Unfortunately, for visitors and locals alike, there are two other unavoidable taxes – an 8 percent tax on food and a 10 percent tax on alcohol.)

Bed & Breakfast is becoming an increasingly popular option in the Toronto area. Many of the homes are in residential neighbourhoods, with hosts who are only too delighted to share their knowledge of the city. The price for two is usually in the $70–$80 range, including parking.

The prices for the hotels have been categorized as follows: **$** = under $100; **$$** = 100-150; **$$$** = 150-200; **$$$$** = over $200. All prices are in Canadian dollars and all are correct at the time of going to press, but do check when making bookings, as they may have changed.

CAMBERLEY CLUB HOTEL (54 rooms)
40 King Street West, 28th Floor
Tel: 947-9025/1-800-866-7666
Fax: 947-0622
The old-world charm is somewhat reminiscent of an English gentlemen's club,

although infinitely more welcoming. On the 28th floor of 68-storey Scotia Plaza, in the heart of Toronto's financial core, spectacular views of Lake Ontario compete with utter elegance and caring service. $$$$

CROWNE PLAZA TORONTO CENTRE (587 rooms)
225 Front Street West
Tel: 597-1400/1-800-HOLIDAY
Fax: 597-8128
A 25-storey tower adjacent to the Metro Toronto Convention Centre, this up-market Holiday Inn property is geared towards the business traveller. The high glass walls and ceiling of its Trellis Bistro & Lounge provide a memorable setting for watching falling snow. $$$

DELTA CHELSEA INN (1,586 rooms)
33 Gerrard Street West
Tel: 595-1975/1-800-268-1133
Fax: 585-4362
Within steps of Yonge Street, it's well-situated for Maple Leaf Gardens, and other downtown attractions. Specializes in programs for children, including a Children's Creative Centre. $$

FOUR SEASONS HOTEL (381 rooms)
21 Avenue Road
Tel: 964-0411/1-800-268-6282
Fax: 964-2301.
The flagship of the international Four Seasons group, this multi-award-winner is one of North America's top hotels, in the heart of fashionable Yorkville. Spacious bedrooms and marble bathrooms; a twice-daily maid service and a high staff-to-guest ratio ensures quality, personalized service. $$$$

HOLIDAY INN ON KING (425 rooms)
370 King Street West
Tel: 599-4000/1-800-HOLIDAY
Fax: 599-7394
Steps from the theatre district and the Metro Toronto Convention Centre, marble and mahogany are the urbane theme of this business-oriented hotel. Excellent views of Lake Ontario and SkyDome from some of the rooms. $$

HOTEL INTERCONTINENTAL (213 rooms)
220 Bloor Street West
Tel: 960-5200/1-800-327-0200
Fax: 960-8269
Wood panelling, gleaming brass and touches of art deco in the lobby, intimately warm but luxurious guest rooms with windows that open, and a charming inner garden courtyard. On the edge of Yorkville, close to Royal Ontario Museum and galleries. $$$$

THE KING EDWARD HOTEL (315 rooms)
37 King Street East
Tel: 863-9700/1-800-225-584
Fax: 367-5515
A historic Edwardian landmark that has graced the Toronto scene since 1903. Its vaulted ceilings, marble pillars and opulent public rooms have recently been restored to their elegance. $$$$

PARK PLAZA HOTEL (284 rooms)
4 Avenue Road
Tel: 924-5471/1-800-268-4927
Fax: 924-4933
A recently restored Toronto landmark in a prime location at the corner of Avenue Road and Bloor, on the doorstep of fashionable Yorkville and two minutes from Royal Ontario Museum. Its Roof Restaurant has been a long-standing favourite with the literati set. $$

NOVOTEL TORONTO CENTRE (266 rooms)
45 The Esplanade
Tel: 367-8900/1-800-221-4542
Fax: 360-8285
A comfortable European-style hotel that's part of a French chain, within minutes of the St Lawrence Market, the financial district, shopping and most major entertainment venues. $$

Elegant street lighting

Family homes offer B & B

RADISON PLAZA HOTEL ADMIRAL
(157 rooms)
249 Queen's Quay West
Tel: 203-3333
Fax: 203-3100
An intimate hotel on Toronto's busy waterfront. Polished brass, lacquered wood and marine art emphasize the hotel's nautical theme – even the rooms seem like spacious cabins. A courtesy shuttle bus service to the downtown core. $$

QUALITY HOTEL (DOWNTOWN)
BY JOURNEY'S END (194 rooms)
111 Lombard Street
Tel: 367-5555/1-800-228-5151
Fax: 367-3470
A no-frills hotel with all the necessary amenities. Minutes' walk from the St Lawrence Market and downtown. $

QUALITY HOTEL (MIDTOWN)
BY JOURNEY'S END (211 rooms)
280 Bloor Street West
Tel: 968-0010/1-800-228-5151
Fax: 968-7765
Across from the University of Toronto, and three blocks from the Royal Ontario Museum and Yorkville, an excellent central location for the budget-minded business traveller. $

RAMADA HOTEL, TORONTO DOWNTOWN
CITY HALL (715 rooms)
89 Chestnut Street
Tel: 977-0707/1-800-854-7854
Fax: 977-1136
A large yet modest hotel in a convenient locale for business and pleasure. Close to City Hall and Nathan Phillips Square, the Eaton Centre and right on the edge of Chinatown. $

ROYAL YORK HOTEL (1,403 rooms)
100 Front Street West
Tel: 368-2511/1-800-268-9411
Fax: 368-2884
Situated over the road from Union Station, this popular Canadian Pacific hotel has been an integral component of the downtown scene since 1929. It is a railway hotel that continues to symbolize tradition, starting in the comfortable lobby with its gleaming chandeliers, fresh flower arrangements and invitingly plump armchairs. $$$

SHERATON CENTRE TORONTO
(1,392 rooms)
123 Queen Street West
Tel: 361-1000/1-800-325-3535
Fax: 947-4854
Practically a city within a city, with over 60 boutiques and immediate access to the 6-mile (10-km) Underground City. Amenities include Canada's largest indoor/outdoor swimming pool and a rambling ¾-ha (2-acre) landscaped garden. There are excellent downtown views from all rooms. $$$

SUTTON PLACE GRANDE HOTEL
LE MERIDIEN TORONTO (280 rooms)
955 Bay Street
Tel: 924-9221
Fax: 924-1778
Quiet attention to detail, original works of art in the guest rooms, and the ambience of Sansouci – the gourmet dining room – all underline the hotel's intent to resemble the grand hotels of Europe. Long a favourite of show biz types, it's also ideal for anyone on (provincial) government business. **$$$**

TORONTO HILTON (601 rooms)
145 Richmond Street West
Tel: 869-3456/1-800-267-2281
Fax: 869-1478
A comfortable, business-oriented hotel in the heart of downtown's shopping district, within easy walking distance of the Art Gallery of Toronto, theatres and concert halls. Exotic Polynesian fare at Trader Vic's. **$$**

TORONTO MARRIOTT EATON CENTRE (459 rooms)
525 Bay Street
Tel: 597-9200/1-800-228-9290
Fax: 597-9211
Perfect location for shoppers, since the hotel is connected to the Eaton Centre. An indoor rooftop pool for a different view of the city. **$$**

WESTIN HARBOUR CASTLE (975 rooms)
1 Harbour Square
Tel: 869-1600/1-800-228-3000
Fax: 869-1420
All the rooms in this lakeside hotel look out over Toronto Harbour and Lake Ontario. There's a relaxing away-from-it-all feel, although it's only minutes from Toronto's financial and cultural core. Spectacular views from the revolving Lighthouse Restaurant on the 37th floor. **$$**

Bed and Breakfast

Three registries representing B & B homes in the downtown area will supply free brochures on request. They are: Bed and Breakfast Homes of Toronto, PO Box 46093, College Park Post Office, 444 Yonge Street, Toronto, Ontario M5B 2L8,

tel: 363-6362; Downtown Toronto Association of Bed and Breakfast Guest Houses, PO Box 190, Station B, Toronto, Ontario M5T 2W1, tel: 690-1724; and Toronto Bed and Breakfast Inc, PO Box 269, 253 College Street, Toronto, Ontario M5T 1R5, tel: 588-8800/961-3676.

Guardians of the law

HEALTH AND EMERGENCIES

In the case of any emergency that requires the police, an ambulance or the fire service, tel: 911. All non-Canadian visitors should purchase health insurance before leaving home. The following telephone numbers may be useful:
Canadian Medic Alert: tel: 696-0267
Dental Emergency: tel: 967-5649
Dental Emergency Service: tel: 485-7121 (9.30am to midnight)
Hospital/Dental Emergencies: tel: 340-3944 (The Toronto Hospital provides 24-hour emergency medical and dental service at 150 Gerrard Street West.)
Hospital and Medical Insurance for Visitors: tel: 961-0666
Credit Cards Lost or Stolen:
American Express: tel: 474-9280 (1-800-221-7282 for lost or stolen traveller's cheques)
Diners Club Enroute: tel: 1-800-525-9135
Mastercard: tel: 232-8000
VISA: Phone the issuing bank.

COMMUNICATIONS AND NEWS

Telephone

The telephone numbers in most of Metropolitan Toronto are preceded by the area code 416. However, area code 905 has recently been added, as the 416 code was becoming overloaded. Some numbers within area code 905 are still considered a local call, others are long distance. If you are calling a long distance number, dial 1 first; if it is not a long distance call, you simply dial 905 and the rest of the number. The long distance information pages at the front of the telephone directory provide information on long distance calls. If you are unsure, call the operator on 0. If you need to find a local number, tel: 1-555-1212. Local telephone calls made from a phone box are charged at standard rate, no matter how long the call may be.

Media

Currently Toronto has four daily English-language newspapers, *The Globe and Mail* and *The Financial Post* (both circulated nationally), *The Toronto Star* and *The Toronto Sun*. Over 300 consumer magazines are published in Toronto, but the two major ones are *Maclean's*, a weekly news magazine, and the monthly *Saturday Night*. National and regional radio and television stations are based in Toronto, including the Canadian Broadcasting Company (CBC) which operates nation-wide networks in French and English for both radio and television, and CTV. There are also many multi-cultural, multilingual broadcast outlets, and 65 ethnic newspapers are published here.

Toronto has two alternative newspapers, *Now* and *Eye*, which provide comprehensive, up-to-date listings on all kinds of entertainment, gallery showings and a wide range of events.

USEFUL INFORMATION

Attractions

There are many other museums besides the ones covered in the itineraries. Black Creek Pioneer Village, on the north-west outskirts of Toronto, is a recreated village in which visitors can stroll through Ontario's past. The Toronto Historical Board operates a number of historical homes that are open to the public, as well as Old Fort York, a recreation of the original settlement. The Hockey Hall of Fame opened in June 1993, on the concourse level of BCE Place – although part of the

collection is in the old (1885) Bank of Montreal building at the corner of Front and Yonge. Already thousands of hockey fans have been able to re-live some of hockey's most memorable moments. The Metro Toronto Zoo is a long trek out, in the Rouge Valley of Scarborough, but well worth the effort. You needn't be deterred by the weather as many of the animals are in huge pavilions such as the Indo-Malayan Pavilion or the African Pavilion. In winter, cross-country skiers combine a tour of the zoo with visits to the pavilions to warm up!

People with Disabilities

The *Guide to Ontario Government Programs and Services for Disabled Persons* is an excellent, free booklet obtainable from the Office for Disabled Persons, 700 Bay Street, Toronto M5G 1Z6, tel: 965-3165 (voice/TDD for people who have impaired hearing).

Children

Kids Toronto is a useful newspaper for parents, giving lists of activities for children. It is available free in bookstores and libraries.

SPORT

Whatever the season, there is always a sporting event to attend. During the winter months, the Toronto Maple Leafs, who are in the National Hockey League (ice hockey, that is) play regularly at the historic Maple Leaf Gardens. During the spring, summer and fall, the Toronto Blue Jays, who are part of the American League, bring baseball to the SkyDome, and the Toronto Argonauts, who play a particularly Canadian-style football, also play at SkyDome. For those more actively-inclined, there's the Martin Goodman Trail, a 22-km (13-mile) jogging and cycling path beside Lake Ontario. In the winter month, skaters can take a spin on the outdoor skating rink at Nathan Phillips Square or down at Harbourfront Centre's York Quay.

USEFUL ADDRESSES

Tourist Offices

THE METROPOLITAN TORONTO CONVENTION AND VISITORS ASSOCIATION (MTCVA)
Suite 590
207 Queen's Quay West
M5J LA7
The office operates a toll-free line, to provide information on places to stay, things to see and do, and special events. Weekdays 8.30am–5pm, Saturday 9.00am–5.30pm, Sunday 9.30am–5pm, tel: 203-2500 for local calls, 1-800-363-1990 for calls from Ontario, Greater Montreal and the continental USA. MTCVA also has information stands at Eaton Centre.

Embassies

CONSULATE GENERAL OF THE UNITED STATES
360 University Avenue
(north of Queen Street)
M56 154
Tel: 595-1700

CONSULATE GENERAL OF BRITAIN
777 Bay Street (corner of College Street)
M56 292
Tel: 593-1267

Visitors from other countries should look in the white pages of the telephone book under 'Consulate Generals'.

FURTHER READING

Adventurous Torontonian's Food Guide, The by J Issenman, Tundra Books, 1989.
Discovering Ontario's Wine Country by Linda Bramble & Shari Darling, Stoddart Publishing Co Limited 1992.
Great Country Walks Around Toronto by Elliot Katz, Great North Books, 1993.
Horsing Around Toronto & Beyond by Helen Mason, Whitecap Books, 1993.
Toronto Architecture – A City Guide by Patricia McHugh, McClelland & Stewart Inc, 1989.
Toronto's Backyard: A Guide to Selected Nature Walks by D Gregory & R MacKenzie, Douglas & McIntyre, 1986.
Toronto Sketches, 'The Way We Were' by M Filey, Dundurn Press Limited, 1993.
The Toronto Story by Claire Mackay & Johnny Wales, Annick Press Limited, 1990.
Toronto Then & Now by J Clarence Duff with Sarah Yates, Fitzhenry & Whiteside, 1984.

Boating on the ice

Acknowledgments

Photography	Ottmar Bierwagen *and*
10	Archive Canada
13	Canadian National Exhibition Archives
11	Sutro Library
12	Toronto Historical Board
14	Toronto Transit Commission
33B	Martha Ellen Zenfell
Handwriting	V.Barl
Cover Design	Klaus Geisler
Cartography	Berndtson & Berndtson
Production Editor	Mohammed Dar